FRONTISPIECE.

Ja.ˢ Sowerby delin.   Ja.ˢ Newton sculp.

London, Publish'd as the Act directs Dec.ʳ 1, 1780 by J. Lavers N.º 10 Strand.

THEORY AND PRACTICE
OF
FENCING

by J. M^CARTHUR of the ROYAL NAVY

The Naval & Military Press Ltd

published in association with

ROYAL ARMOURIES

Published by
The Naval & Military Press Ltd
Unit 10 Ridgewood Industrial Park,
Uckfield, East Sussex,
TN22 5QE England
Tel: +44 (0) 1825 749494
Fax: +44 (0) 1825 765701
www.naval-military-press.com

in association with

ROYAL ARMOURIES

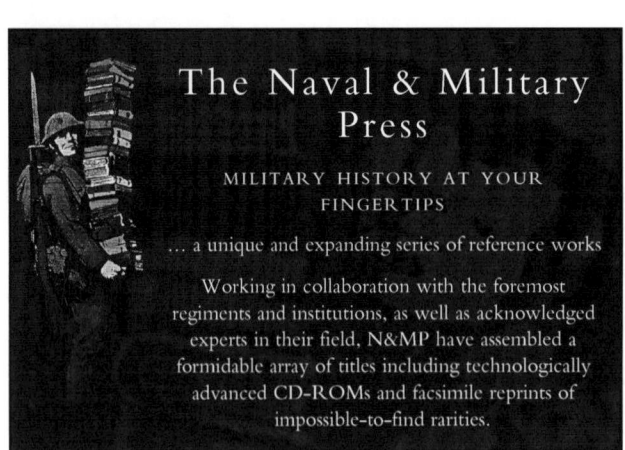

In reprinting in facsimile from the original, any imperfections are inevitably reproduced and the quality may fall short of modern type and cartographic standards.

Printed and bound by Antony Rowe Ltd, Eastbourne

TO

HIS GRACE JOHN DUKE OF

ARGYLL,

&c. &c. &c.

MY LORD DUKE,

WHEN I did myself the honour of presenting the manuscript copy of the following Treatise to your Grace, about two years ago; I did not then foresee that it would have remained so long unpublished;

but

DEDICATION.

but the unsettled line in which I am placed, and the necessary attendance to the duties of my department, have in a great measure been the cause of impeding the publication. However, I have now the satisfaction to think that the work is rendered more perfect, by several additional improvements which, I hope, will also meet with your Grace's approbation.

There are few, or none, besides your Grace, to whom I could with so much propriety dedicate a work of this nature. For your Grace is not only possessed of that inherent love to the Arts and Sciences in general, and to Arms in particular, which

have

DEDICATION.

have always so nobly distinguished your Grace's ancestors; but also, possessed of an innate desire to promote and encourage them, which has, in a particular manner, illustriously distinguished your Grace's character. It would be vain in me to follow the common tract of dedicators, by launching forth into a panegyrick on your Grace's many qualifications; as all the encomiums my feeble pen could bestow, are already sufficiently known to the world. It would be equally vain to swell this dedication with a panegyrick on Fencing, or the utility thereof; as that is sufficiently known to your Grace.

DEDICATION.

That your Grace may long enjoy health and happiness, to promote and encourage the Arts and Sciences, is the sincerest wish of,

MY LORD DUKE,

Your Grace's most obedient,

most devoted, humble Servant,

JOHN M°ARTHUR.

LONDON, 2d December,
1780.

PREFACE.

FROM an early period, I made the study of the Art of Fencing my principal amusement, when it did not interfere with any other study. My chief instructions I received in the course of eighteen months lessons, from M. Herault, sometime assistant teacher of the Royal Academy at Paris: since that time, have visited several Academies and Schools for Fencing, and found masters differ materially in their mode of teaching. I must here express my partiality in preferring Mr. Olivier's manner of giving lessons, to any that I have seen, either

PREFACE.

either in London or elsewhere; which, perhaps, may arise from the principles he lays down, coinciding nearly with those which I was taught.

The motives that principally induce me to publish the following Treatise on the Theory and Practice of the Art of Fencing, are, because such Treatises as I have perused, have been published by Professors, or Teachers of that art, and are incomprehensible to young learners; owing to the intricate manner they have made choice of, in describing the different movements, parades, and thrusts, which should be rendered as simple and easy as the nature of the Art would admit; so that young learners might acquire a perfect knowledge of the Theory of Fencing, and be

PREFACE. vii

be enabled to execute, or put the same in practice, with little or no instructions from masters.

The treatises hitherto published, are entirely calculated for such persons as have made a proficiency in Fencing; and not for gentlemen, who might only have the opportunity of a few months lessons. They may indeed be of use to the former, by having recourse to them occasionally, in order that they may recal to their memory what might be acquired during former practice; but can avail little to such gentlemen, as have only been superficially grounded in the principles of the Art.

It

It is certainly the interest of masters, to intersperse their publications with some intricacies; otherwise by making the art too facile, it might prove prejudicial to them in their profession.

I must confess, that Mr. Olivier, in his Treatise, has reduced the art to more simple and natural movements than any other Professor; but it is not so methodically arranged, nor so explicit, as a learner could wish. The representation of the attitudes are in many respects erroneous and unnatural, both with regard to the posture of the body and position of the hands and feet. But that might have been the designer's fault.

PREFACE.

In the following Treatise, I have been at some trouble in adopting the plan of constructing mathematical figures, for the further illustration of the various lessons on the parades, which I have endeavoured to render as plain and easy as possible. I believe it will be found a mode entirely new; and I hope, esteemed an additional improvement to the Art. It may, perhaps, pave the way for some expert mathematician, (having a good knowledge of the theoretic part of fencing) to reduce every principle and movement of the art to proper mathematical demonstrations, which will at once make the study of this art both useful and agreeable

PREFACE.

I flatter myself, that proficients in fencing will find many things new in the following sheets; and young learners, who have a genius for the art, with the assistance of two, or at most, three months lessons from a master, will be enabled to acquire a thorough knowledge of it, so as to put all their parades and thrusts in execution, when entering upon assaults or loose play. I will allow, that a great deal of practice is absolutely necessary, before a young learner can execute all his parades and thrusts with that ease, agility, and justness necessary; but, by strict attention to the rules I have laid down, after receiving the rudiments thereof from a master, he may acquire justness and agility in fencing, equally as much

PREFACE.

much by practising these parades and thrusts with a learner, who has made similar progress, as if he practised them with a master; always observing to execute every manœuvre with minute exactness; and to prevent his contracting erroneous habits, to have frequent recourse to the lessons and instructions here laid down.

INTRODUCTION.

THE Art of Fencing has of late years been universally cultivated in most parts of Europe.—In the East Indies, the art has been always peculiarly esteemed and cultivated by all ranks of people.—These European Fencing-masters skilled in the art, meet with every encouragement that their most sanguine hopes could have formed.

In England the art is now held in greater repute than ever, and is universally introduced as a necessary branch of military education. Some people indeed (from false prejudices) object against the cultivation of this art, as tending to inspire the possessor with an improper share of confidence, animation, and false courage, leading him into broils and quarrels, generally terminated by the

the cuſtom of duelling. But theſe objections are ſoon obviated, when it is conſidered, that very few of the many who devote themſelves to the practice of duelling underſtand a ſingle movement in fencing ; for piſtols are the deciſive weapons generally made uſe of on occaſions of this nature. It muſt therefore be aſcribed to the quarrelſome diſpoſition, and perhaps, too ſtrict notions of honour imbibed by duelliſts, and not to any knowledge they might derive from the acquiſition of this art.

The juſt application of the Theory and Practice of this art, can never be viewed in a diſadvantageous light by liberal minds. On the contrary, many advantages are derived from the proper cultivation thereof. For it not only inſpires the poſſeſſor with a competent ſhare of manly confidence and animation, at the ſame time producing an eaſy and graceful manner; but, conſidered only as an exerciſe, it has the peculiar qualities over every other, of being conducive to the moſt agil motions, the moſt graceful attitudes, a bold and martial air, ſuſceptibility of feeling, quickneſs of

INTRODUCTION.

of fight, and withal, is particularly conducive to the improvement of health and muscularity of body. The study of it, in a scientific manner, tends to constitute a powerful invention, a quick conception, a penetrating judgment, and lively imagination.

For the cultivation of the military and manly exercises, the ancients instituted their Olympic and Pythian games.—In some parts of Europe and the East Indies, a custom does at present prevail of judges presiding annually, and distributing premiums to the most skilful practitioners in the various branches of Fencing. This, while it excites a noble emulation in the breasts of youth, serves as a basis to the real execution of military operations.

It is to be regretted, that a method is not adopted in our Royal Navy, of exercising the ships company of frigates, and such small vessels of war as are liable to be boarded, with simple Fencing, in the stile of *broadsword*

sword play *, (commonly called cudgelling) as it would be of the utmost utility in the offensive and defensive attacks of boarding. This might easily be accomplished, by making it a branch of the duties of a master at arms qualified, to exercise the crew, or such of them as might be allotted for boarding, in the rudiments of the art; and from the spirit of emulation prevailing among them, they would soon make themselves proficients, by a little practice.

Where commanders have introduced and encouraged this exercise among their ship's company, singular advantages have ensued in the action of boarding sword in hand, both with respect to the safety of their men, and capture of the enemy; a particular instance of which we have had this war, in the action of one of his Majesty's armed cutters with *two French privateers*, both of superior force; when, after having met with powerful resistance in boarding and capturing one of

---

* The guards and cuts used in broad-sword play, are the same to be used with a cutlass, hanger, &c.

them, after the other had ftruck, not a man was flain, though feveral of the enemy fhared that fate.*

We find in antient hiftory, that in the cultivation of military exercifes, the right hand or left were employed as occafion might require, without partiality to either; particularly in the Grecian and Roman armies, felect parties of the moft expert foldiers were formed as *ambidexters*, fit to act upon any emergency.

It is a matter of wonder, that a cuftom from which many advantages might refult in clofe attacks, fhould in modern times be entirely abolifhed; when, by confining our obfervations only to the navy, we may at once perceive the utility of cultivating *ambidexterity*, amongft the company of fuch fhips as are liable to be boarded, whether armed with pikes, cutlaffes, poll-axes, piftols, &c.

---

* The gallant commander forefeeing the advantages that might refult from cudgelling, had previoufly encouraged this exercife, by fupplying the crew with bafket-guards and cudgels.

Should thefe letter obfervations appear rather digreffive and difinterefting to fome readers, it is hoped they will be thought worthy of a place, when their utility in the practical application are confidered.

To attain a degree of eminency in any art or fcience, a knowledge of the moft extenfive *Theory* muft be acquired and judicioufly applied to *Practice*.—Hence the art of Fencing, as well as every other military art and fcience, muft be founded on a theory of juft principles, progreffively digefted and combined, without which we never can attain perfect knowledge of any art. Numberlefs inftances might be quoted from the antient as well as modern hiftories of the fuperior excellencies and advantages arifing from a well grounded theory over practice, experienced by the foldier, navigator, and others, in their various profeffional arts. But to draw a full comparative view of thefe would be foreign to this work, and exceed the bounds of an introduction.—However, it is beyond difpute, that a combination of both Theory and Practice is equally neceffary in every military art, as the various fhades in the art of painting are to the expreffion of the fubject.

CONTENTS

PART I.

Of the GUARDS and SIMPLE PARADES and THRUSTS in general

	Page
LESSON I. *THE Manner of holding the Sword or Foil; common Guard of Carte, and of the Advance*	3
—— II. *Of the Guard in Tierce, Advance and Retreat thereof*	7
—— III. *Of the Two simple Parades or Parries of Carte and Tierce*	8
—— IV. *Of the Two simple Parades of Semicircle and Octave*	11
—— V. *Of the Two simple Parades of Second and Prime*	15
—— VI. *Of the Extension and Longe, Thrusts of Carte, Carte over the Arm, and Tierce*	20
—— VII. *How to thrust Low Carte, Octave and Flanconnade*	24
—— VIII. *How to thrust Seconde and Prime*	28
—— IX. *Of engaging and disengaging*	31
—— X. *Of the practical Variations on engaging and disengaging, advancing and retreating, simple Parades and Thrusts of Carte and Tierce*	33

CONTENTS

LESSON XI. *Of the simple practical Variations on the Parades and Thrusts of Semicircle and Low Carte* - 37

———— XII. *Of the simple practical Variations on the Parades and Thrusts of Octave and Flanconnade* - 41

———— XIII. *Of the simple practical Variations on the Parades and Thrusts of Prime and Seconde* - - 46

PART II.

On the various COUNTER PARADES, COUNTER DIS ENGAGEMENTS, FEINTS, GLIZADES, &c.

LESSON I. *Of the Salute in Carte and Tierce, and of the ornamental Parades and Thrusts of Tierce and Carte, sometimes called Thrust at the Wall* - 53

———— II. *Of the counter or round Parades in Carte and Tierce* 61

———— III. *Of the circle Parade, and of the counter Parade in Octave* - - - - - - 65

———— IV. *Of the counter Parades in Prime and Seconde* 68

———— V. *Of the counter Disengagements of Carte and Tierce, and natural Thrusts* - - - - 71

———— VI. *Of the counter disengagements in Semicircle and Octave, and natural Thrusts* - - - 73

LESSON

CONTENTS.

	Page
LESSON VII. *Of the counter Disengagements in Prime and Seconde, and natural Thrusts*	74
——VIII. *Useful practical Lesson on the Parades and Thrusts of the counter in Carte and Tierce*	76
——— IX. *Of the practical Variations on the counter Parades and Thrusts of Carte and Tierce*	78
——— X. *Of the practical Variations on the counter Parades and Thrusts in Semicircle and Octave*	82
——— XI. *Of the practical Variations on the Counter Parades and Thrusts of Prime and Seconde*	86
——— XII. *Of the different Feints*	91
——— XIII. *Of the Cuts over the Point, Thrust of the Wrist, Return of the Wrist, and Return on the Extension, &c.*	94
——— XIV. *Of Appels or Beats with the Foot, Beats on the Blade, and Glizades*	97
——— XV. *Of the Time Thrust, and practical Variations thereon*	99
——— XVI. *Of the practical Variations on the different Feints*	104
——— XVII. *Of the practical Variations on the Cuts over the Point, &c.*	108
———XVIII. *Of the practical Variations on the Thrust of the Wrist, Thrust of Extension, &c.*	111
——— XIX. *Of the practical Variations on Appels, Beats on the Blade, and Glizades*	115

PART III.

Of ASSAULTS and ATTACKS in general; containing some useful Observations on the Time Thrust, the most advantageous Manner of attacking an Adversary either out of Measure or in Measure; also Rules and Observations on single Combat with Swords; and the most eligible Method of disarming an Adversary in Fencing with a Foil, or in serious Affairs with a Sword 123

LIST of the PLATES.

		Page
PLATE I.	*Common Guard of Carte*	4
——— II.	*Parade of Semicircle*	12
——— III.	*Mathematical Illustration of the simple Parades of Carte and Tierce, Semicircle and Octave*	14
——— IV.	*Parade of Seconde formerly called Quinte*	16
——— V.	*Position of Extension*	20
——— VI.	*The Longe and Thrust of Carte*	22
——— VII.	*Parade of Octave*	42
——— VIII.	*Return on the Extension after parrying with Octave the Thrust of Low Carte*	44
——— IX.	*Salute previous to thrusting Tierce and Carte*	54
——— X.	*Parade and Thrust of Carte*	58
——— XI.	*Mathematical Illustration of the simple Parades of Prime and Seconde, also the counter Parades of Carte and Tierce*	64
——— XII.	*The Parade of Octave against the Thrust of Low Carte*	66
——— XIII.	*Mathematical Illustration of the counter Parades of Octave and Semicircle, also Prime and Seconde*	70

PLATE

LIST OF THE PLATES.

PLATE XIV. *The Parade of Semicircle against the Thrust of Seconde* - - - - 82

———— XV. *Time Thrust upon an Adversary's Motion of disengaging to Tierce* - - - 100

———— XVI. *Guards upon joining Blades for an Assault* 124

———— XVII. *The Time Thrust in Carte upon an Adversary's Motion to cut over the Point* - - 130

————XVIII. *Parade of Prime against the Force in Tierce, or Thrust of Carte over the Arm* - - 140

———— XIX. *Disarming by crossing the Sword* - - 156

ERRATUM.

In PAGE 112. LINE 14. for *Plate* 10. read *Plate* 18.

PART I.

Of the Guards and simple Parades and Thrusts in general.

THE art of fencing with foils or small-sword play may be reduced to two principal guards, and six simple parades and thrusts; from which every other parade and thrust is derived. These may be justly termed the basis of every movement in fencing; and the learner should first of all, know how to execute them, with minute exactness, before he proceeds to their compounds: for if he wants to acquire knowledge and execution in fencing in a scientific manner, he must proceed progressively to learn, step by step, in the order of the following lessons, without which he can never acquire that execution and firmness so necessary to make a good fencer. The different salutes in fencing, which are never used in academies but when going to thrust tierce and carte, or previous to an assault, shall be treated of in their proper places: therefore the first thing to be learned is,

LESSON I.

The Manner of holding the Sword or Foil. Of the common Guard in Carte; and of the Advance on said Guard.

IN order to hold your sword well, the hilt must be flat in your hand; so that the two edges will be nearly horizontal when you throw yourself upon guard; your thumb stretched along upon the upper flat part of the hilt, within half an inch of the shell, and the pummet is to rest under your wrist. Having hold of your sword or foil in this manner, and standing upon your first position, which is similar to what is called the third position in dancing, that is, your right foot before the left, with the heel advanced near to the buckle, throw yourself upon the common guard of carte, by advancing your right foot about the distance of a measured foot and an half from the left, or at the distance of two lengths of your own foot from the heel of the other.—The two heels should be in the same straight line. Turn your wrist in such manner, that the nails may appear upwards. Your hand should be on a line with the lower part of your breast; the arm not stretched, but a little bent and flexible, and the elbow inclined a little to the outside. The point of your sword or foil should be about fifteen degrees elevated, and nearly fixed on a line with the upper part of your adversary's breast. *See plate 1. of the attitude, also plate 3. fig. 1. and references.* The left arm (which is necessary to balance the body in its different movements) must be raised in a semicircular manner, on a line with the forehead, the hand kept open in an easy manner, the thumb and first finger nearly meeting. Your body should be totally sideways, and your head turned towards the right, so as to keep sight of your point; for it is evident, the less you expose the breadth of your body, by keeping it in a direct side posture, the more difficulty there will be to touch you in assaults: your body, feet, arms and shoulders, should be in the same straight line: let the balance of your body rest upon the left leg, by keeping the left knee bent and flexible, so as you may incline a little backwards; the right leg should be kept easy on the

ground

Common Guard of Carte.

ground, the knee alſo a little bent and perpendicular to the point where your right heel reſts. *See plate* 1.

Having made ſure of the poſition above directed on carte guard, you muſt now, with the utmoſt regularity, learn to advance and retreat upon this guard, without varying your poſition; to do which with ſteadineſs and regularity, requires ſome degree of attention in the beginning: for ſure there is no art that calls for ſuch minute (I may ſay mathematical) exactneſs as this. Unleſs the poſitions in every leſſon are ſtrictly adhered to, the learner may fall into irregular habits, that may for ever after obſtruct his progreſs in fencing. In order to advance with regularity, move the right foot with eaſe forward to the diſtance of more than a foot, making the left foot inſtantly follow to the ſame diſtance; theſe two movements muſt ſeem as one, by being comprehended in the ſame moment of time. Keep your body firm and ſteady upon guard while advancing. Let there be a pauſe of time, as long as a perſon might count three, between every advance, always obſerving, after making five or ſix advances, that the diſtance and poſition of your guard is exactly the ſame with your primitive

diſtance

distance and position. The retreat on this guard is performed in the same manner as the advance thereon, only your left foot makes the first movement backwards, and your right follows in a line of direction at the same moment.

This is the first guard naturally taken by beginners, when entering upon assaults; and from it in general all the various thrusts and parades are thrown.

The other guard, called tierce, is taken in assaults for the most part by experienced fencers; which I shall treat of in the following lesson.

LESSON II.

Of the Guard in Tierce; Advance and Retreat thereof.

THE position of this guard is the same with that of carte. The hand only must be a little reversed, so as that the nails, which were upwards in carte, must be half turned downwards, when in tierce-guard. The arm should be a little stretched outwards, in order to cover or secure the outside. The point should be in the same direction, as if on the other guard of carte; that is, fixed steadily, that your eye may perceive it opposite to the upper part of your adversary's breast. Advance and retreat on this guard with the same ease and regularity as done in carte, agreeable to the instructions given in the first lesson.

LESSON III.

Of the two simple Parades or Parries of Carte and Tierce.

THESE parades are commonly distinguished from the others, by their securing or covering the breast from all thrusts made towards it; hence are generally called, by way of distinction, *upper parades*. To perform the simple parade of carte, place yourself on the common guard, according to *lesson* 1. *plate* 1. and with a firm hold of your foil, throw your hand towards the left, (which I call inwards) the distance of about six inches from guard, making a gradual turn upwards with the wrist, in order to throw off your adversary's blade with the greater ease; at the same time drawing your hand a little towards your body, that the opposition formed may feel more powerful. Though your wrist and hand are both moved in performing this parade, yet to perform it with more exactness, the point of your foil,

body

body and legs, should be in the same direction as if on guard. *See plate* 3. *fig.* 1. *and references thereto.*

The simple parade of tierce is also performed from the common guard, by keeping a firm hold of the foil in your hand, throwing and stretching your arm obliquely downwards to the right (or outwardly), the nails being reversed downwards, by the gradual turn of the wrist, in forming the parade. It parries the simple thrust of carte over the arm and seconde. The distance of the hand upon this parade from common guard, is also six inches, consequently the distance between the covered parades of carte and tierce should be twelve inches obliquely. The point of your sword should not deviate from the line of direction in forming compleatly either parades: as further illustrated by *plate* 3. *fig.* 1. *and references.*

REFERENCES to Plate 3. Fig. 1.

A B. DIRECTION of blade and point in the medium or common guard of carte, elevated to fifteen degrees nearly. *C. B.* The direction of blade and point in having formed the parade of carte. *D. B.* The direction of blade and point, in forming the parade of tierce. *A. C.* The gradual afcent or diftance inwards, from the common guard to the parade of carte. *A. D.* Gradual defcent or diftance outwards, from guard to the parade of tierce, each being fix inches from *A.* the common guard. Hence from *C.* to *D.* or in other words, from the parade of carte to the parade of tierce, is twelve inches, and *B.* is the angular point.

LESSON IV.

Of the two Parades of Semicircle and Octave.

SEMICIRCLE parade, so called from the points forming a curve resembling a half circle in its course upon performing it, from the guard of carte, is a very safe and useful parade against the thrusts of low carte and seconde. *See plate* 18. Also against the disengage and thrust of carte over the arm. In order to perform it well, your body must be steadily inclined upon the left side, appearing quite sideways.—Drop your point with the nails turned upwards, so as to form an angle of nearly forty-five degrees with the guard point. *See plate* 3. *fig.* 2. At the same time, stretch your arm well out, raise the hand as high, or on a line with your mouth, and your arm thrown inwards, the distance of six inches, from the line of direction in your common guard, that your point may appear to the eye in looking over your arm. *See plate 2. of the attitude.* Alfo *plate 3. fig. 2. and references.*

The octave parade is naturally ufed after, and performed contrarily to the parade of femicircle. In performing octave and femicircle alternately, the courfe of the point fomewhat refembles the figure of eight.

It is, without exception, the beft and moft ufeful parade in fencing, when well formed; it is alfo the moft difficult parade to execute; as it requires fuch an amazing flexibility in the wrift, which few can attain to, without a great deal of practice.—Its utility I fhall mention more fully, when I come to treat of the counter parades and affault.—To perform it well, you muft raife the hand the height of your chin, the nails not turned up fo much as in femicircle; your arm well ftretched, and thrown outwards, the diftance of fix inches; the wrift fhould be bended as much as poffible, in order that the point may fall on a line with your

adverfary's

Parade of Semi-circle.

adverfary's flank, making nearly the fame angle from guard point as femicircle. *See plate* 7. *of the attitude.* alfo *mathematical illuftration in plate* 3. *fig.* 2. *with references.*

The difficulty young learners find in performing this parade, arifes from the wrift's being neceffarily bended, when the arm is raifed and ftretched, in order that the point may be properly dropt, and fixed on the line of direction.

REFERENCES to Plate 3. Fig. 2.

A B. Inclination of blade and point in the common guard of carte. *A. C.* direction of blade and point, when you drop to the parade of femicircle.—*D. C.* direction of blade and point, in covering yourfelf inwards, or forming compleatly the parade of femicircle. *E. C.* Direction of blade and point, in forming compleatly the parade of octave.—The outward arc *B. C.* is formed by the point in its courfe from *B.* in dropping to the

parade

parade of femicircle. The inward arc *B. C.* contrarily to the other, is formed by the point dropping from guard to the parade of octave.—*A. D.* the gradual afcent or diftance inwards, upon forming the compleat parade and oppofition in femicircle.—*A. E.* the gradual defcent and diftance outwards, in forming compleatly the parade of octave.—*D. E.* The gradual defcent and diftance from the covered parade of femicircle, to the covered parade of octave, equal to twelve inches, and *E. D.* the contrary.

Remark. The diftance of the hand between thefe two covered parades, is equal to the diftance between the two parades of carte and tierce.

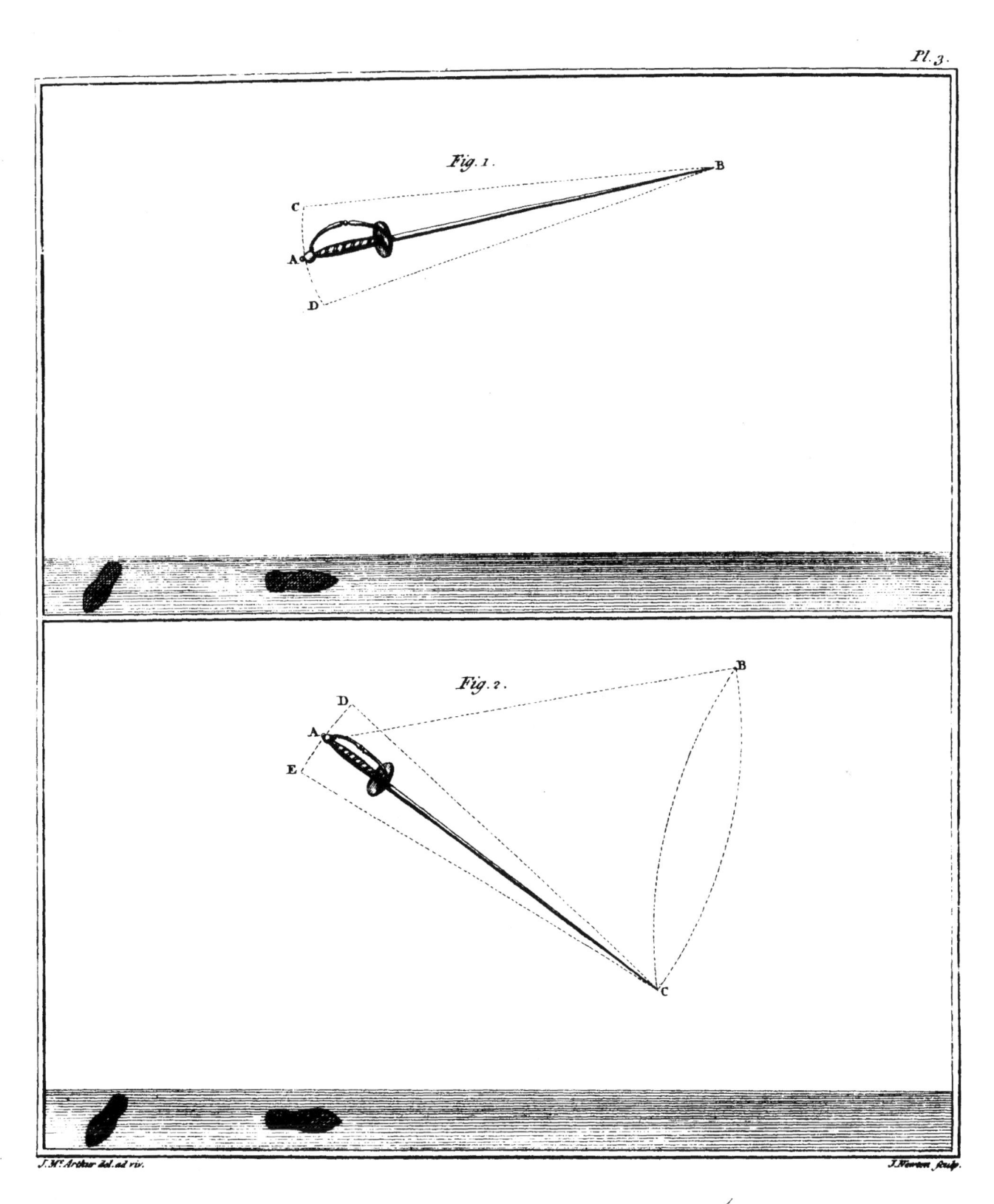

Mathematical Illustration of the Simple parades of Carte & Tierce; Semicircle & Octave.

London Publish'd 1 Dec.r 1780, by J. Lavers N.o 10 Strand.

LESSON V.

Of the two Simple Parades of Seconde, (formerly called Quinte) and Prime.

THESE two parades are not put in use so frequently as the other four, though I have generally observed that young learners entering upon the assault, naturally betake themselves to throwing of seconde parade almost against every thrust, which may arise from its being so easy to execute.

The parade of seconde is very powerful against the simple thrusts of low carte and seconde. If well formed and strongly thrown, must give you an opening to touch your adversary on the return. It is for the most part performed, either from the guard of carte or tierce,

and

and sometimes after the parade of prime, to prevent your adversary from counter disengaging on that parade.

To perform it from carte or tierce, the nails and wrist should be reversed downwards, the point dropped, and the hand opposed outwards as in the parade of octave. The point's tract from guard is also nearly the same with the parade in octave, and the inclination of the blade should form the angle of forty-five. *See plate* 4. *of the attitude, also mathematical illustration in plate* 11. *fig.* 1. *and the references.*

Prime parade is performed with the nails reversed downwards, the hand raised higher than your mouth, opposed inwards, in the same manner as semicircle. The arm should be drawn well in towards your body, and the wrist bended downwards, that the point may fall more than in any other low parade.

I object to the method used by a number of teachers in performing this parade, that is, by keeping

the

Parade of Seconde, formerly call'd Quinte.

London, Publish'd Dec.r 1, 1780 by J. Laver, N.º in Strand.

the point in a more horizontal direction than they do in any other low parade. For the principal use thereof is, to parry your adversary's thrusts, when endeavouring to force in upon you, being engaged in tierce, and advancing within his measure; makes it absolutely necessary to drop your point ten or eleven degrees more than in semicircle, or any other low parade. *See plate* 11. *fig.* 1. *and references.*

To perform seconde parade from prime, is only throwing the hand with a gradual descent from the inward position of that parade, till you are covered outwards by seconde parade. Hence the movement of the hand from the one parade to the other, and the gradual ascent and descent thereof, is similar to the movement, ascent, and descent of the hand, in executing the parades of octave and semicircle, with this variation, that here the wrist is reversed and raised higher in prime. For further illustration, *See plate* 11. *fig.* 1.

REFERENCES to Plate II. Fig. 1.

A B Direction of blade and point in the common guard of carte *A C* Direction and inclination of blade and point, in dropping to the parade of prime, agreeable to the above leſſon. *D C* Elevation of the hand, and inclination of the blade and point, after forming and covering yourſelf in prime parade. The outward arc *B C* is the courſe of the point from carte or tierce, in forming ſaid parade. *A E* Direction of blade and point in dropping to the parade of ſeconde. *F E* Direction of blade and point, in forming compleatly ſaid parade of ſeconde. The inward arc *B E* courſe of the point from guard, to the parade of ſeconde. *A D* the gradual aſcent and diſtance inwards, upon forming the compleat parade of prime. *A F* the gradual deſcent and diſtance outwards, in forming the parade of ſeconde.—*F D* or *D F* the gradual aſcent or deſcent of the hand from one covered parade to the other.— Hence the diſtance from prime to ſeconde, is nearly the equal to the distance from semicircle to octave, only as before observed, the nails are reversed downwards.

Having treated thus far of the two guards, and six different simple parades; I shall now regularly proceed to treat of the different simple thrusts used in fencing; and conclude *Part* I. by laying down some practical variations upon all these different parades and thrusts.

LESSON VI.

Of the Extension, Longe, and Thrusts of Carte, Carte over the Arm, and Tierce.

THRUSTS are for the most part executed with the longe, except thrusts of the wrist, and thrusts of the extension. They may be performed, either after disengaging the point or not, just according to circumstances. *Engaging and disengaging is treated of in lesson 9th.*—To perform the straight thrust of carte inside; your point must be well fixed to your adversary's breast, the arm well raised, and opposed inside, the nails upwards, your body projecting forward; by steadily forming your extension of the right arm and left leg. *See plate 5.*

The

Position of Extension.

London, Publish'd Dec.3, 1780 by J. Lavers N°.11, Strand.

The extenfion is a moft effential part of the longe, as it affifts in directing and fixing your point with vivacity to your adverfary's body. The learner fhould always advert to form his extenfion previous to longeing; and by dint of a little practice, he will naturally make the extenfion and longe comprehend the fame moment of time; for if, on the contrary, he accuftoms himfelf to longe without having formed the extenfion, his body and point will always waver, and feem infirm; befides, it will obftruct his quicknefs in delivering the thruft, and in recovering.

So foon as you have formed the above pofition of extenfion, pufh home with vivacity the thruft in carte, by longeing out to the proportional diftance of your height. If a perfon of middling ftature, the diftance of the right foot from the left fhould not exceed four feet, but more, if the perfon is very tall. Or by another rule, which I think more preferable, the diftance of a compleat longe fhould be equal to twice the diftance of your guard. Your left arm, upon every longe, is

ftretched

stretched down by the flank, at the distance of two or three inches, and always raised as you recover upon guard, by way of grace and balance to your movements.—Your body should incline a little forwards; the head raised upright, looking outwards over the shoulders, so as to have a full view of the point. As you approach your adversary's breast, you make a gradual resistance against his foil inwards, by way of cover to your longe. This is commonly called the opposition in thrusting carte inside. The right knee bent, and in a perpendicular posture with your heel; the left knee and ham stretched, with the foot firmly fixed to the ground. *See plate* 6.

To recover with ease and quickness from your longe to guard, requires a little practice; the only instructions I can give concerning it, are, to lean with some degree of force on the heels of both feet; the greatest force is first upon the right, then it falls on the left; by bending the left knee at the same time, and inclining the body backwards, you come to guard.

The

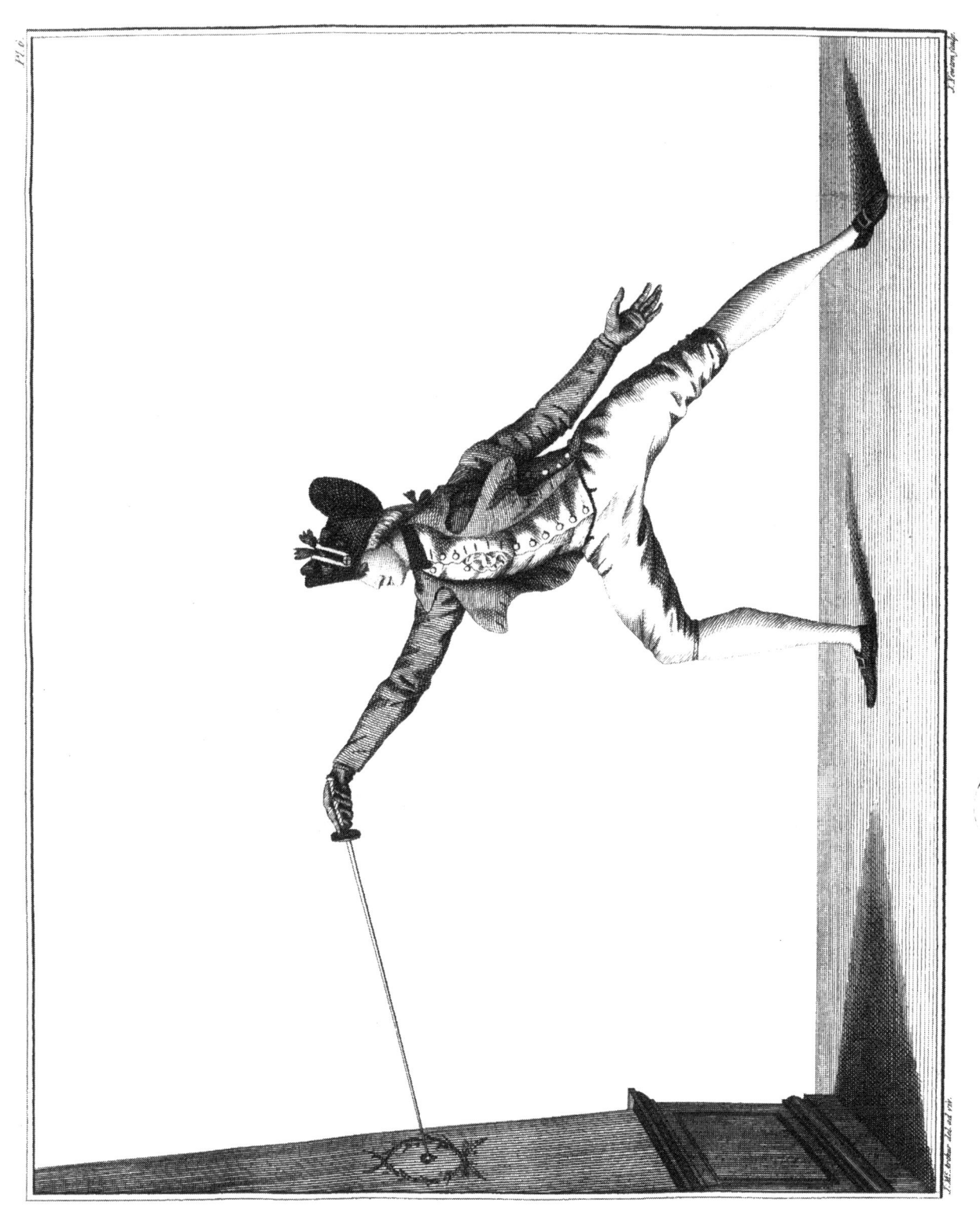

The Lunge and Thrust of Carte.

London Publish'd Dec.r 1, 1780 by J. Hawes, N.o 10 Strand.

The thrust of carte over the arm, is performed in the same manner as carte inside, by disengaging to tierce; with this difference, that the head is raised upright in the inside, and the hand well opposed outwards, in order to be well covered.

The thrust of tierce is rather awkward to use in assaults or attacks. It may be thrown in with safety, when your adversary holds his hand low, being engaged in tierce. It differs only from carte over the arm, by reversing the wrist, the hand being also well raised and opposed outwards.

LESSON VII.

How to thrust Low Carte, Octave and Flanconnade.

LOW carte, sometimes called semicircle thrust, is naturally delivered after forming the parade of semicircle, in the same manner as simple carte thrust; only the hand and point must be fixed lower. *See plate* 12. It may be used against your adversary on various occasions, either with feints or otherwise: Such as making movements, as if intending to push for the breast; but deceive him, by delivering a quick thrust on the belly. It is an excellent thrust, and seldom fails to hit your adversary, if he has frequent recourse to his high parades. I shall treat of it more fully in the practical lessons.

Octave

Octave thruft is for the moft part, by generality of mafters improperly blended with the thruft of low carte; tho' in fact, it is a diftinct and feparate thruft of itfelf, and the oppofition contrary to low carte.—It is naturally delivered after the parade of octave, on the flank or belly; the arm being well oppofed outwards. If you parry your adverfary's thruft by octave, your return will naturally be the thruft of octave, which may at the fame time touch him with the extenfion only, independent of the longe. *See plate* 8.

This thruft is liable to the fame variations, as the thruft of low carte or femicircle, and may be delivered with the greateft fafety on the engagement of tierce, by dropping your point under the wrift of your adverfary, that moment delivering the thruft with a good oppofition outwards. *See practical variations, leffon* 12. *alfo plate* 12.

Flanconnade may with propriety be united to octave, as it is performed when engaged in carte, by abruptly

binding

binding your adverfary's blade, in feizing forcibly the feeble of it; at the fame time drop your point under his wrift, fixing it to the flank, cover yourfelf outwards, and thruft home octave.—The left hand is generally ufed in oppofition to your adverfary's blade and point, as there may be fome danger of running upon it, unlefs your octave is exceedingly well oppofed. Therefore, would recommend the learner to draw his left hand, with the back turned towards his breaft, when longeing in flanconnade; that he may thereby oppofe, or throw off his adverfary's blade, if the point is like to approach him. However, if the oppofition in octave is well formed, there is no neceffity for the above precaution.

Flanconnade is furely a dangerous thruft in affaults, if not very cautioufly ufed. Your judgment and obfervation muft direct when to throw it moft favourably. Unlefs octave thruft and oppofition is nicely formed, it expofes you to the time thruft from your adverfary.—The moft favourable occafion for delivering this thruft, I always found on the engagement of carte,

when

when an adverfary keeps his wrift and point low; then is the time to bind his blade, and throw in your thruft as above directed. For further illuftration, *See practical variations, leffon* 12.

LESSON VIII.

How to thrust Seconde and Prime.

THE thrust in seconde is naturally delivered after the parade of tierce, or when engaged in tierce by dropping the point under your adversary's wrist, the nails reversed downwards, as in the parade of seconde, then longe and deliver the thrust on the flank or belly.—Advert that the arm should be well opposed outwards, and the head held upright inwards. *See plate* 14.

Prime is the natural thrust in return, after having parried your adversary's force, when advanced considerably within his measure, and pressing vigorously upon you.

It is only an extension of the arm from the opposition of the parade to your adversary's body, the
nails

nails being kept reversed downwards.—The position of the arm differs from the position thereof in seconde, by being well raised and opposed inwards. *See lesson 5.*

In prime thrust, there is seldom occasion for making the longe, as your adversary is supposed to have attempted forcing in upon you, and advanced for that purpose considerably within his measure, so that the extension of the arm, or to be more sure (the compleat extension) must infallibly reach his body, if there is an opening.—This is the distinction I would make between the thrust of prime and seconde. There is, perhaps, some novelty in it, as the generality of masters make no distinction, but comprehend prime thrust in seconde, which, I beg leave to think, is quite erroneous; for they might, with the same propriety confound the two parades together, though the opposition of the one is inwards, and the other outwards

There may be various favourable occasions for executing effectually, all the foregoing parades and thrusts.

The

The moſt material variations that thoſe ſimple parades and thruſts are liable to, I have laid down in the following practical leſſons, which every learner ſhould frequently exerciſe, as they tend to make him acquire firmneſs, eaſe, and agility in fencing.

But, previous to entering upon the practical variations, it is neceſſary the learner ſhould underſtand Engaging and Diſengaging, as in *leſſon* 9.

LESSON IX.

Of Engagiug and Disengaging.

ENGAGING in carte or in tierce, is to oppose your adversary's blade, either inside or outside, when you first join or cross blades on guard. *See plate* 16.

To engage in carte, by joining or opposing blades inwards, is by far more easy than tierce engagement for a young practitioner; it being less difficult to execute therefrom, the different disengagements and feints in pursuing his designed thrusts.

But, the engagement of tierce, by joining blades outwards, is certainly the best in every respect for a proficient; as from it he has an opportunity of executing the best subtle feints, of being better secured or covered

on

on his intended thrufts, and of making ufe of the favourite parades of the counter in tierce, octave, &c.

Difengaging or caveating, is performed by dextroufly fhifting the point of your fword or foil from one fide of your adverfary's blade to the other; that is from carte to tierce, or *vice verfa*.—It is one of the moft neceffary motions in fencing, and upon the dextrous performance of which depends the fuccefs of your intentions againft an adverfary, with fubtle feints, &c.

To perform it well, either from carte or tierce, let the foil be eafy in your hand, with the point flightly preffed towards the fort or ftrength of your adverfary's blade; then with an eafy and flexible movement of the wrift only, difengage or fhift your point clofely to the other fide.

Pleafe to obferve, that the arm fhould not deviate from the line of direction, as the difengagement muft intirely proceed from the flexible motion of the wrift.

LESSON X.

Of the practical Variations on Engaging and Disengaging, Advancing, and Retreating, simple Parades and Thrusts of Carte and Tierce.

NOW, suppose you are engaged in carte with an adversary, who (properly speaking) should be one skilled a little in fencing (if a master so much the better), for the more ready compliance to your movements in the practical lessons;

1st. He retreats, you advance, well covered in carte, *See lesson* 1.—He retreats again, you may advance with a disengagement to tierce, and so forth, alternately, taking care that you are properly covered on each engagement: his retreat and your advance should be comprehended in the same moment of time; in the same manner, you may retreat while he advances.

2d. On the engagement of carte, your adversary delivers a straight thrust in carte; oppose it by forming your parade in carte, then return the straight thrust thereof.

3d. He again thrusts straight in the same manner, also throw it off by forming your parade in carte, deliver in return the thrust of carte over the arm, by disengaging to tierce.

4th. On the same engagement he retreats while you advance, then execute the whole movements of the second branch of this lesson.

5th. On the same engagement, retreat while he advances. Execute the movements in branch third.

6th. On the same engagement, he disengages to tierce, and thrusts carte over the arm; throw it off by

forming

forming your simple parade in tierce, then make a quick return of the thrust of tierce. *See lesson 6.*

7th. On the same engagement, he retreats, you advance; he then disengages and thrusts carte over the arm, throw it off by forming your parade in tierce, and if he keeps his wrist low in recovering, deliver him a return in tierce; if not, disengage and thrust carte inside

8th. On the same engagement, he advances with a disengagment, retreat and form your parade in tierce; disengage as he recovers, and deliver a thrust in carte; he throws it off by his parade of carte, makes a return by disengaging to tierce; parry it also by forming tierce, and deliver a quick return of the thrust, carte over the arm.

9th. On the engagement of tierce, he disengages and thrusts carte inside, throw it off by forming your parade in carte, disengage, and thrust carte over the arm; he parries it, and makes a return in tierce, which you throw off by forming said parade of tierce, then longe home with a straight thrust in tierce.

10th. On the engagement of carte, he forces or presses hard upon your blade; then disengage nimbly, and deliver the thrust of carte over the arm.

11th. On the same engagement, he again forces upon your blade, disengage and thrust carte over the arm; he throws it off by forming the parade in tierce, and delivers a straight thrust, which parry with tierce; then disengage and deliver the thrust of carte over the arm.

12th. On the same engagement, he in like manner forces upon your blade; disengage to tierce, and form your extension; he comes to form his parade in tierce, then nimbly disengage again, and deliver the thrust of carte inside. These two disengagements, when performed quickly, are called feints *une deux*, or feints, *one two*, which I shall treat of largely in the lessons on feints, counter disengagements, &c. *See part 2d.*

Re-

Remark. The three last branches of the above lesson may be performed from the engagement of tierce, making the disengagements, parades, and thrusts, correspond to the side engaged upon.

LESSON XI.

Of the simple practical Variations on the Parades and Thrusts of Semicircle and Low Carte.

BRANCH first. On the engagement of carte, drop your point, and deliver the thrust of low carte according to *lesson* 7.

2d. On the same engagement, your adversary thrusts carte straight home; throw it off with your parade of carte, then deliver a return of the thrust in low carte.

3d. On the same engagement, disengage to tierce, and thrust carte over the arm; he opposes it with his parade, and returns a disengaged thrust in carte; which throw off with the parade of carte, then with vivacity drop your point, and deliver a thrust in low carte.

4th. On the same engagement, repeat all the movements of the last branch; then he makes a return in low carte, throw it off by recovering, quickly forming the parade of semicircle; and conclude this branch by returning a thrust in low carte.

5th. On the same engagement, he disengages in order to thrust carte over the arm, throw it off by forming your parade in semicircle, return a thrust in low carte, which he parries with semicircle, and in return delivers a thrust in carte; oppose it with your simple parade of carte, make your extension as if going to push high; but in place thereof, when he comes to form his high parade, drop your point, and thrust low carte.

6th. On

6th. On the same engagement, disengage to tierce; he comes to use his parade in tierce, disengage again to carte, and deliver him a thrust in low carte.

7th. Repeat the movements of the last branch, and after having disengaged to carte, you may form your extension, as if intending to push high, then quickly deliver the thrust in low carte.

8th. On the engagement of tierce, he forces upon your blade, disengage and deliver your thrust in low carte.

9th. On the same engagement, repeat the same movements, he throws off your thrust by his parade of semicircle; then as he recovers, after you parry his return, deliver him a thrust over the arm.

10th. On the engagement of carte, he advances, disengages and delivers a thrust in tierce, while at the same time you retreat, forming the parade in tierce;

tierce; on his recovering he forces upon your blade, then difengage and return low carte.

11th. on the fame engagement, he retreats while you advance, then difengage and thruft carte over the arm; he parries it, and thrufts in return, by difengaging to carte, throw it off by forming your parade of carte, and thruft carte ftraight home; he oppofes it, by forming the parade of carte. If he is flow in making a return, or that his hand deviates from the line of direction as you recover, deliver him a thruft with the wrift in low carte. *See leffon on the thrufts of the wrift, Part 2.*

12th. On the engagement of tierce, you may repeat all the movements of branch 9th, except the laft therein, then difengage compleatly over the arm, and deliver your thruft in octave, forming a good oppofition againft his blade outwards.—I have enlarged upon his laft difengagement in *Part 2. leffon 6. and 9.*

Remark.

Remark. It is in a master's option to vary the above lesson considerably, by introducing the most material branches of the practical variations in *lesson* 10th.

LESSON XII.

Of the simple practical Variations on the Parades and Thrusts of Octave and Flanconnade.

BRANCH first. On the engagement of tierce, drop your point, and deliver your adversary a thrust in octave, observing to form a good opposition. *See lesson* 7.

2d. On the engagement of tierce, your adversary by disengaging attempts to deliver a thrust in low carte, you throw it off by forming the parade of octave. *See lesson 7. and plate 12.* Then make a quick return of the thrust in octave. N. B. This is, without exception, one of the best parades, and return in fencing against such thrusts; for if your opposition is well formed, and point well directed, you may at the same moment, before he has time to recover, touch him on the flank. But in assaults it requires practice and attention, to execute it with that nicety necessary, so as to touch your adversary upon the longe the same moment the parade is formed.

3d. On the engagement of carte, you may repeat the movements of branch 2d.

4th. On the same engagement, he disengages to tierce and thrust, throw it off by your parade of tierce; then reverse your nails upwards, and return a thrust in octave.

5th. On

Parade of Octave.

London, Publish'd Dec.r 1st 1780, by J. Hayes No. the Strand.

5th. On the same engagement, he thrusts low carte; oppose it, by forming your parade in semicircle, then deliver a thrust in octave, by disengaging over his arm; commonly called a counter disengagement.

6th. On the same engagement, repeat all the movements of the last branch, then he opposes your thrusts in octave, by forming his parade; if he makes a return, by disengaging over the arm to low carte, oppose it by your parade in semicircle, and deliver a thrust in low carte.

7th. On the same engagement of tierce, he disengages and delivers a thrust in low carte; oppose it by forming your parade in octave, then disengage compleatly over his arm, and deliver your thrust in low carte.

8th. On the same engagement, he makes a thrust either straight in teirce or in carte over the arm; oppose it by forming the parade of tierce, make an extension of the arm as if intending to return the same thrust, but by way of deception, drop your point, and thrust octave.

9th. On the engagement of carte, bind your adverfary's blade, by abruptly feizing it with yours; drop your point under his wrift, and thruft octave.—This is called the thruft of flanconnade. *See leffon 7.*

10th. On the fame engagement, he thrufts carte; throw it off by forming your parade in carte; and if he recovers with his wrift low, deliver him a thruft in flanconnade.

11th. On the fame engagement, mark the feint of flanconnade, by binding his blade a little, as if you intended to deliver him that thruft, but in place thereof, deliver him a ftreight thruft either in carte or low carte.

12th. On the fame engagement, he thrufts carte, oppofe it by forming your parade, then as he recovers mark feint flanconnade as above; if he oppofes or forces upon your blade at the time, nimbly difengage to tierce, and deliver the thruft of carte over the arm.

The Return on Extention after parrying with Octave your Adversary's thrust.

13th. On the same engagement, he delivers the thrust in flanconnade, oppose it strongly by forming the parade of octave, and deliver him octave thrust quickly in return.

14th. On the same engagement, he thrusts low carte, parry it forcibly by octave, at the same instant forming your extension, fix your point well to his body, and you must inevitably touch him at the same time. *See plate* 8.

LESSON XIII.

Of the simple practical Variations on the Parades and Thrusts of Prime and Seconde.

BRANCH first. On the engagement of tierce, your adversary advances within his measure, and with violence delivers a thrust in tierce or carte over the arm; do not retreat, but oppose his blade by forming the parade of prime. *See lesson* 5. and *plate* 18. afterwards return a thrust in prime. *See lesson* 8.

2d. On this same engagement, he advances, disengages, and forcibly thrusts carte, drop your point also, and parry it with prime; then disengage over his arm, and return a thrust in seconde.

3d. On

3d. On the engagement of carte, he difengages and thrufts carte over the arm, parry it with fimple tierce, and return a thruft in tierce; he advances as you recover within his meafure, forcing upon your blade, form your parade in prime, and deliver a quick return of the thruft thereof.

4th. On the fame engagement, he again difengages, and thrufts carte over the arm, which parry with tierce and return the thruft thereof; he forces a thruft without advancing, parry it with prime, then difengage over the arm, and return your thruft in feconde.

5th. On the engagement of tierce, he delivers a thruft in feconde; throw it off by forming the parade thereof, as in *leffon* 5. then deliver a quick return as he recovers, by thrufting feconde; as in *leffon* 8.

6th. On the engagement of carte, he delivers a thruft in low carte; oppofe it with the parade of feconde, and deliver a return thereof, as in laft branch.

7th. On the same engagement, he disengages and thrusts carte over the arm, parry it with simple tierce, and deliver a quick return of the thrust in seconde.

8th. On the same engagement, disengage your point, as if going to thrust carte over the arm, he will naturally betake himself to the simple parade of tierce, then nimbly reverse your wrist, and thrust seconde.

9th. On the engagement of tierce, drop your point under his wrist, as if intending to thrust seconde; then nimbly reverse your nails upwards, and deliver the thrust of carte over the arm.

N. B. This is called feint seconde, carte over the arm. *See lesson 2. in part 2. concerning feints.*

10th. On the same engagement, advance and force upon his blade, he opposes it with prime, and returns the thrust, which you must endeavour to parry, by quickly recovering and forming your parade in prime.

11th. On the engagement of carte, force upon his blade, he gives you an opening in tierce, disengage and thrust carte over the arm with vivacity; he parries it with simple tierce, and continues leaning upon your blade; then as you recover, make a quick thrust of the wrist in seconde.

12th. On the same engagement, deliver him a thrust in low carte, he parries it with seconde, and returns the thrust thereof; oppose it also by the parade in seconde; and he will naturally expect a straight return from you, deceive him, by disengaging over his arm, and deliver the thrust in seconde. *See part 2. on Counter Disengagements.*

Remark. It is necessary the learner should conclude the different branches of the foregoing practical lessons, with the movement of thrusting to his adversary's body; as it conduces in making him acquire steadiness in fixing his point, and firmness upon his longe.

The learner's taste and judgement may make some additional variations to those above laid down; always observing that the different parades, thrusts, and movements should be formed and executed according to nature,—avoiding every superfluous and complex movement, which only tends to obstruct his progress in attaining speedy knowledge of the art.

PART II.

ON

THE VARIOUS COUNTER PARADES,
COUNTER DISENGAGEMENTS,
FEINTS, &c.

PART II.

LESSON I.

Of the Salute in Carte and Tierce, and of the Ornamental Parades and Thrusts of Tierce and Carte, (sometimes called Thrust at the Wall).

TO thrust tierce and carte, by engaging and disengaging alternately to your adversary's breast, while he opposes you by separately forming his simple parades of tierce and carte, may be justly called the Beautiful Emblem of Fencing.—Every learner should frequently

frequently exercife this leffon, of parrying and thruft-ing tierce and carte.—You may perhaps at firft, not comprehend the ufe and advantage thereof, as it is feemingly very fimple and eafy to execute.—But the frequent practice of it, contributes greatly in making you acquire a proper and noble pofition on guard, nimblenefs and nicity in executing your difengagements, and withal firmnefs and fteadinefs in longeing and recovering.—In a word, it is the beft rudiments of the art, and by which every proficient is, at firft fight, enabled to judge of the progrefs or abilities in fencing of different adverfaries.

You fhould never begin to thruft tierce and carte, without previoufly going thro' the eftablifhed cuftom of faluting; which is performed as follows:

Being on guard, engage your adverfary's blade on the outfide; by way of compliment, defire him to thruft firft at you, then drop your point, by reverfing the nails well downwards, with a circular motion;—

draw

Salute previous to exercising the Ornamental Parades & Thrusts of Tierce & Carte.

draw your right foot close behind the left, near the buckle, stretching both hams, raising your right arm; and with your left hand, take off your hat gracefully;— then make a circular motion with your wrist, reversing the nails upwards, while you advance your right foot forward, forming your extension. *See plate* 9. Your adversary makes the same motions, keeping equal time with you; but in place of forming the extension, he makes a full longe, as if going to thrust carte inside, in order to take his measure; presenting his point at a little distance from your body, while you remain uncovered on the extension. *See plate* 9. When your adversary recovers, after having taken his measure, you also recover by drawing the right foot or heel close to the heel, or near the buckle of the left; the right hand well stretched and raised, the nails upwards, and the point dropped; the left hand raised in a semi-circular form, as if on guard, your hat held therein with ease and gracefulness; the head held upright, and the hams stretched. In this attitude, salute first in carte, by forming the parade thereof; then salute in tierce, by

forming

forming the parade of tierce: Laſtly, make a circular motion with the wriſt, by dropping your point in tierce, that moment puting on your hat, and throwing yourſelf upon the guard of carte.

When it is your turn to puſh, the ſalute only differs in one particular from the above; that is, in place of forming the extenſion, and uncovering the body, you make a full longe from the firſt poſition of the right foot behind the left, in carte; then recover to the ſecond poſition, by placing the right foot or heel cloſe to the heel of the left; and conclude with the other movements.

All the motions of the above ſalute ſhould be performed deliberately with eaſe and grace, not with any degree of precipitation, as the generality of maſters teach.

After performing the ſalute, and being engaged in carte; your adverſary, agreeable to the compliment offered,

fered, pushes at your breast by disengaging nimbly to tierce, and thrusting carte over the arm.

Please to observe, that the wrist is never reversed when he disengages; oppose it by forming the parade of tierce, with the most minute justness. *See lesson* 3. *part* 1. Then drop the point, by way of accustoming yourself to make the return in seconde, which may be termed the grace on the parade of tierce. Remain on this grace till your adversary recovers to guard. So soon as he has recovered to guard, join his blade in tierce; he disengages by thrusting carte inside; throw it also off by forming the parade of carte with minute exactness. *See plate* 10. *also lesson* 3. *part* 1. The grace or ornament to be used after forming this parade, while your adversary is upon the longe, is done by allowing the foil to remain flexible in your hand, with the point downwards, keeping your hand in the same direction, as if covered upon the parade. Or if this grace is tiresome to the arm, you may vary it by drawing the arm a little in towards the body, after parrying; and allow the blade to fly off outwardly in an oblique manner, by keeping a flight hold of the handle thereof, between the thumb and the two first fingers.

The position of your hand and blade should be so, as you can see your adversary's body thro' the angle formed by your arm and blade, without moving your head or body.

Your adversary, after pushing tierce and carte alternately during pleasure, makes a motion for you to thrust, by commencing the salute, and uncovering his body on the extension, while you take the measure, by longeing in carte as above.

Having joined blades in carte, keep your arm a little bent and flexible, then nimbly disengage, form the extension, *See plate* 5. and with a longe, thrust carte over the arm. Fix your point well to his breast, and form a good opposition. Keep your foil neither too firm nor too easy in your hand. The hand should be susceptible to a
kind

The Parade and Thrust of Carte.

kind of feeling, fo as when your adverfary parries, the blade may fly off obliquely inwards towards your body, the arm not deviating from the line of direction. This laft movement may be termed the cover or grace on the longe of carte over the arm. Previous to recovering upon guard, obferve, whether or not you are firm and fteady on the longe, and all your movements done with exactnefs.

I would not have you accuftom yourfelf always to remain balancing your body on the longe, as by it you may contract a ftiff and bad habit, which will prevent your recovering upon guard with that eafe and fwiftnefs neceffary.

Again, he joins your blade in tierce, difengage nimbly and thruft carte infide. He oppofes it, by forming the parade in carte, *See plate* 10. then let the blade and point fly loofely over the hand, having hold of your foil between the thumb and two firft fingers, by which you will have a view of your adverfary through the angle

made

made thereby. This is the grace upon the longe of carte infide.

For your more fpeedy progrefs in fixing your point, and executing the movements of the thrufts in tierce and carte; I would recommend you to exercife it frequently at the wall, by fixing thereto a wafer, or any other fmall object, about breaft high. Take the proper guard and diftance in carte, make the motion of difengaging, fixing your point on the extenfion, and thrufting home to the object. *See plate* 5. *and* 6. This will infallibly improve a learner.

LESSON II.

Of the Counter or Round Parades in Carte and Tierce.

THE counter parade in carte, is esteemed one of the most essential in fencing when engaged on the guard of carte. It baffles a variety of thrusts, throws off with ease the disengagements over the arm, feints one, two, cuts over the point, &c.

In order to perform it well on the engagement of carte, your adversary disengages; follow his blade or point closely, with a small circle, proceeding entirely from the motion of your wrist, which brings you to join his blade always in carte. If he makes a thrust with the disengagement, oppose it, by gradually covering yourself with the parade of carte, after having followed his

his blade round. It requires a little practice to execute it with any degree of nicety.

The course of the point in forming this counter parade is shown in *Plate* 11. *fig. 2. and references.*

The counter or round parade in tierce, is rather difficult at first to execute, tho' I am of opinion it is superior to the other in utility, when engaged in tierce; and as I before observed, none but such as have made great proficiency in fencing, think it proper to enter upon this engagement in assaults. On that engagement, it parries the disengagements, feints, cuts over the point, &c. made to carte inside.

It is performed in a similar manner to the counter parade of carte, only the course of the point is reversed.—For example, your adversary disengages to carte, with a view to thrust carte inside; follow his blade closely, with a small circle made by the motion of the wrist reversed in tierce, stretching your arm,

and

and giving his blade a smart and abrupt throw off, as you overtake, or meet it in tierce.

Please to observe, that the course of the point in forming the counter in carte is inwards from left to right, and in the counter parade of tierce, the contrary. *See plate* 11. *fig.* 2. *and references.*

Remark. In performing the counter in tierce, throw your head well back, as there may be some danger in bringing the point of your adversary's foil to your eyes, unless the circle is quickly executed.

REFERENCES to Plate 11. Fig. 2.

A B Direction of blade and point in the common guard of carte. *C B* Direction of blade and point, in forming the parade of carte. *D B* Direction of blade and point in forming the parade of tierce. *B E F* The proportional circle formed by the point in executing the counter parade of carte. *B F E* course of the point, in forming the counter parade of tierce.

Observe

Obferve, that in performing thefe counter parades with mathematical minutenefs, the diameter of the circle formed by the courfe of the point, may be fuppofed equal to *A C*, or *A D*, the diftance from common guard to either parades. Therefore, as the diftance *A C* or *A D* is equal to fix inches, alfo equal to the diameter; fo is the circle made by the point, equal to about nineteen inches. This fhould be the wideft circle formed by the point, in executing thefe counter parades compleatly againft any thruft. But fhould be confiderably contracted and reduced in baffling feints or difengagements.

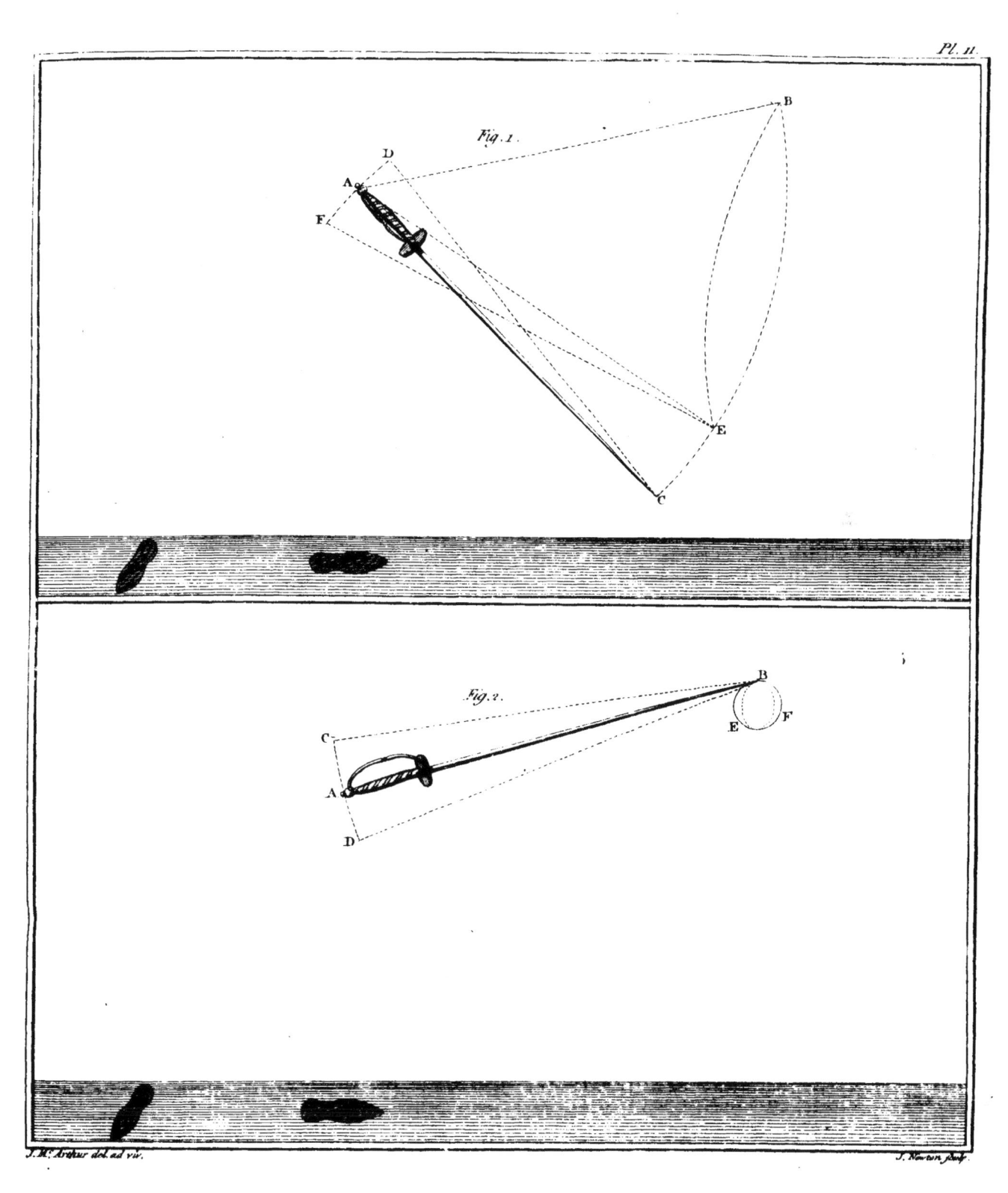

Mathematical Illustration of the Simple parade of Seconde & Prime; Also the Counter parade of Carte & Tierce.

London, Publish'd 1 Dec.r 1780, by J. Lavers No. 10 Strand.

LESSON III.

Of the Circle Parade, and of the Counter Parade in Octave.

THE circle parade, sometimes called doubling semicircle, is esteemed the best of the low parades, when on the engagement of carte. It baffles a variety of your adversary's feints or disengagements, prevents counter disengaging; and should be used when he doubles.

To perform it, your body must be quite sideways, inclining well backwards; the arm raised to the height of your mouth, dropping the point as in semicircle; then by the motion of your wrist, form an exact circle with all possible quickness. *See plate* 13. *fig.* 1.

The counter parade in octave is performed contrary to the circle, the hand in the same position as in simple octave. *See lesson 4. part* 1.

Though the course of the point is contrary to the course thereof in the circle parade, yet it should form a circle of the same magnitude with the other. It is surely more difficult to perform than the other. Skilled fencers frequently make use of it in assaults, when engaged in tierce. It baffles the same variety of feints, disengagements, &c. that the circle parade does on carte engagement; besides, it is the best parade of any, for making a quick return after. *See plate* 13. *fig.* 1. *and references.*—Also *plate* 8.

REFERENCES to Plate 13. fig. 1.

A B direction of blade and point in dropping to semicircle, or to the circle parade. *C B* direction of blade and point, in covering yourself inwards, and forming compleatly the circle parade. *D B* direction of

The parade of Octave against the thrust of Sour-carte.

of blade and point, in forming compleatly the counter parade in octave. *B F E* courſe of the point in the circle parade. *B E F* courſe of the point, in forming the counter parade of octave.

In theſe parades the diameter of the circle formed by the point, may be alſo ſuppoſed equal to the diſtance between the hand dropped in ſemicircle and the parade of octave. Therefore, as the diſtance *A C* and *A D*, are each ſuppoſed equal to ſix inches, alſo equal to the diameter; ſo may the circles formed by the point in executing theſe parades, be ſuppoſed equal to about nineteen inches.

LESSON IV.

Of the Counter Parades in Prime and Seconde.

THESE two counter parades are rather aukward in execution, and of little use to a fencer, that can execute the others with any degree of judgment; however, for method's sake, I shall say something of them.

The counter parade in prime may be used, when your adversary forces in on the engagement of tierce, and attempts to counter disengage. It is performed by dropping the point, nearly as low as in simple prime, forming the counter parade by a circle, proceeding from the motion of the wrist.

The

The counter parade in feconde, is performed by dropping the point, having the hand in the fame pofition as in fimple feconde. *See part* 1. *leſſon* 5. then form a circle contrary to the counter parade in prime. *See plate* 13. *fig.* 2. *and references.*

Remark. In preference to thefe two counter parades, I would advife, if your adverfary counter difengages in prime, immediately to form your parade of feconde, and if he counter difengages in feconde, form your fimple parade of prime. *See practical leſſons.*

REFERENCES to Plate 13. fig. 2.

A B direction of blade and point, in dropping to prime. *C B* direction of blade and point, in forming the oppofition and compleat counter parade in prime. *B G F* the courfe of the point, in forming the counter parade in prime. *A D* direction of blade and point in dropping to feconde. *E D* direction thereof, and defcent of the hand in forming the counter parade and oppofition in feconde. *D H I* the courfe of the point in forming faid parade. Therefore, as the diftance *A C* or *A E* is fuppofed equal to fix inches,—alfo equal to the diameters; fo is the circle *B G F* and *D H I* formed by the point, equal to about nineteen inches.

Fig. 1.

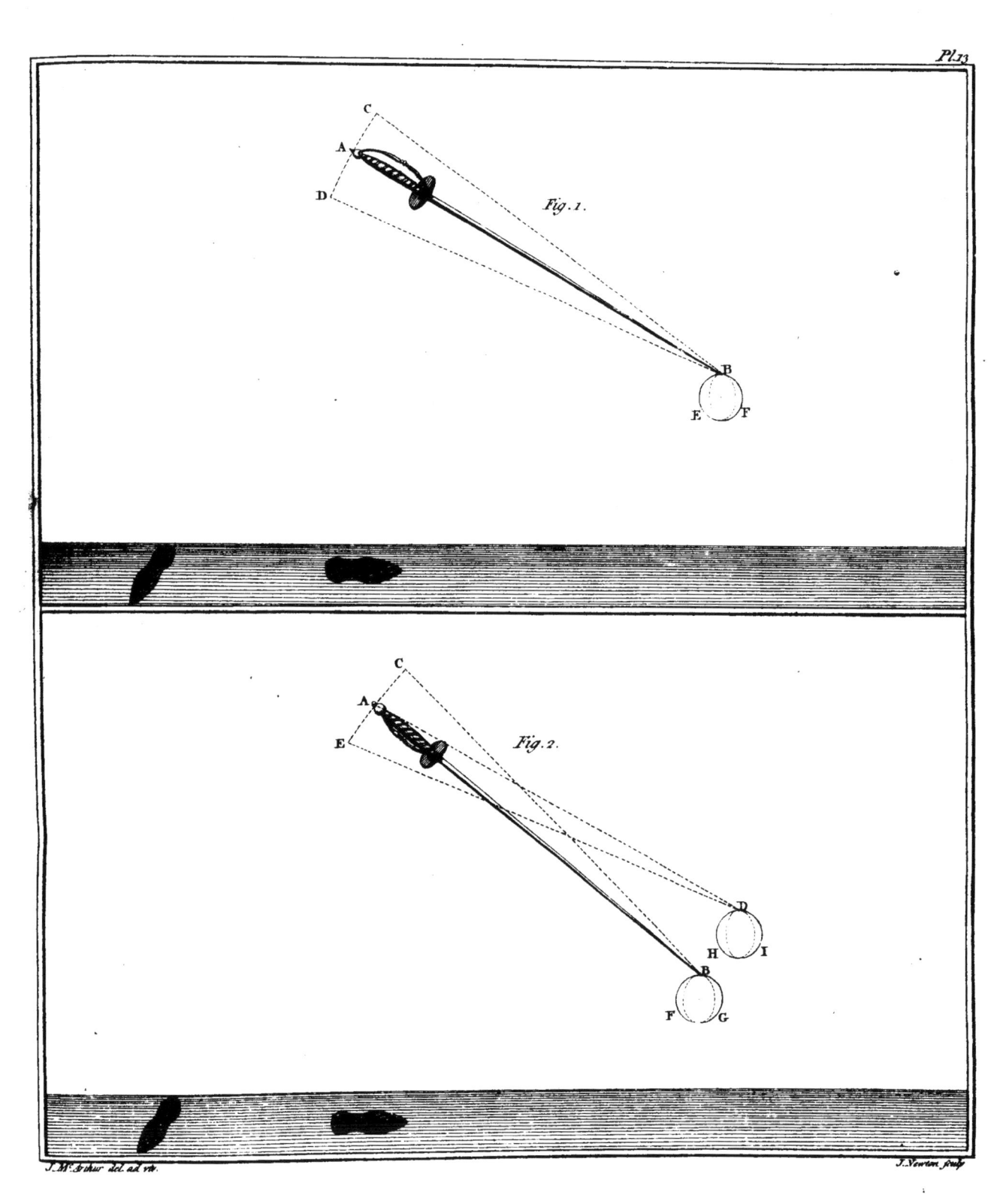

Fig. 2.

Mathematical Illustration of the Counter parades of Semicircle & Octave, Prime & Seconde.

London, Publish'd Dec. 1, 1780 by J. Lavers N°. 10 Strand.

LESSON V.

Of the counter Disengagements of Carte and Tierce, and natural Thrusts of the same.

COUNTER disengagements over the arm, are performed by disengaging from the engagement of carte to tierce, while your adversary opposes it, by forming his counter parade in carte; then nimbly disengage a second time over his arm, and deliver your thrust. It consists of two separate disengagements: and please to observe, that the arm should be well stretched on the first disengagement; nay, if you can manage and balance your body properly, it may not be amiss to form your extension at the same time; which will cause your point to approach nearer his body; so that

that it will be a difficult matter for your adverfary to oppofe it, by a fecond counter parade.

The counter difengagement of cart infide, is performed when you are engaged in tierce, and perceiving that your adverfary will make ufe of his counter parade in tierce. Firft difengage to carte, gradually ftretching your arm towards your adverfary's body; or you may form the extenfion, he at the fame time oppofes it, by forming his counter parade in tierce; then nimbly difengage a fecond time, and deliver your thruft of carte infide.

LESSON VI.

Of the Counter Disengagements in Semicircle and Octave, and natural Thrusts.

THE counter disengagement in semicircle is performed on the engagement of carte, when your adversary accustoms himself to take the parade of semicircle; by first making a feint, as if you meant to thrust low carte, which he attempts to parry with semicircle, then nimbly disengage over his arm, and deliver your thrust in octave.

The counter disengagement in octave, is used for the most part on the engagement of tierce, when you perceive your adversary inclines to parry with simple octave. It is performed by first making a feint, as if you intended

tended to thrust octave, he naturally opposes it, by forming his parade in octave; then nimbly disengage over his arm to carte inside, and deliver either that thrust, or the thrust of low carte.

LESSON VII.

Of the Counter Disengagements in Prime and Seconde, and natural Thrusts.

THE counter disengagement in prime is seldom or never used in attacks; but being so nearly related to prime parade and thrust; I shall, for order's sake describe it. It is performed from the engagement of tierce, by forcing on your adversary's blade,

if

if he betakes himself to the parade of prime, then nimbly disengage over his arm, and deliver your thrust in seconde.

The counter disengagement of seconde, may be more frequently used; and is performed from the engagement of carte, by dropping your point, or making a feint as if you intended to thrust prime.—Your adversary opposes it by forming the parade of seconde; then disengage over his arm, and deliver your thrust by longeing in prime.

LESSON VIII.

Useful practical Lesson on the Parades and Thrusts, of the Counter in Carte and Tierce.

ON the engagement of carte, disengage and thrust carte over the arm; your adversary opposes it, by forming the counter parade of carte. Upon your recover, he in return disengages and thrusts carte over the arm; oppose it by forming your counter parade in carte, &c. disengaging and parrying alternately, always adverting to make your compleat longe with the thrusts, and recover compleatly to guard, while forming the counter parades. Make your movements very slow and exact in the beginning, gradually quickening them as much as possible.

In the same manner, you may exercise on the engagement of tierce, first by disengaging and thrusting carte inside, which he opposes, by forming the counter parade in tierce; in return, he disengages and thrusts carte inside, which parry with the counter parade in tierce, &c. thrusting and parrying as above, 'till you quicken your movements with all possible exactness.

This lesson should be frequently exercised, as it contributes greatly in making you acquire quickness and execution in recovering, counter parrying, &c.

LESSON IX.

Of the practical Variations on the Counter Parades and Thrusts of Carte and Tierce.

BRANCH first. On the engagement of carte, your adversary disengages and thrust carte over the arm; throw it off, by forming the counter parade of carte, then deliver the return of a straight thrust in carte.

2d. On the same engagement, he disengages and thrusts carte over the arm, parry it also by the counter in carte; then disengage, and deliver your return by thrusting carte over the arm.

3d. Repeat

3d. Repeat the movements of the 2d branch; but he parrys your thrust of carte over the arm by the counter parade in carte, then he returns the thrust in carte; which parry with simple carte, and return the disengaged thrust of carte over the arm.

4th. On the engagement of tierce, he disengages and thrusts carte inside, which throw off by your counter parade in tierce; then return a straight thrust in tierce.

5th. On the same engagement, he again disengages to carte; oppose it by your counter parade in tierce, nimbly disengage as he recovers, and thrust carte inside.

6th. Repeat the movements of the 5th branch; but he opposes your thrust in carte, by the counter parade in tierce, and returns a straight thrust in tierce, which oppose by the simple parade thereof; then nimbly disengage, and thrust carte inside.

7th. On

7th. On the engagement of carte, he disengages over the arm, which parry by your counter in carte; then deliver a return of the counter, or double disengaged thrust over the arm;—that is, if he betakes himself to the counter parade in carte at your first disengagement; you must disengage a second time, and deliver the thrust. *See lesson 5.*

8th. On the same engagement, counter disengage, or double carte over his arm; he throws simple tierce in place of a seconde counter parade; then deceive him, by disengaging to carte, and thrusting inside.

9th. Reverse the movements of the two last branches of this lesson, by using the counter parades, while he counter disengages, &c. And besides, in order to prevent him from disengaging to carte inside, as in the conclusion of branch 8th, form your counter parade in tierce, immediately after the counter in carte.

10th. On

10th. On the engagement of tierce, he difengages to carte infide, which parry by the counter in tierce, then deliver a return of the counter difengaged thruft of carte infide. *See leffon* 5.

11th. On the fame engagement, counter difengage, or double to carte infide; while he, in place of forming a fecond counter parade in tierce, forms fimple carte; then, quickly difengage, and thruft carte over the arm.

12th. On the fame engagement, he counter difengages, while you parry with the counter in tierce; and in order to baffle compleatly all his difengagements, you may form the counter parade of carte immediately after the counter parade of tierce.

Remark. The counter parades, and counter difengagements of carte and tierce, are liable to many more variations;—but the above I thought the moft effential.

LESSON X.

Of the practical Variations on the Counter Parades and Thrusts of Semicircle and Octave.

BRANCH first. On the engagement of carte or tierce, if your adversary delivers a thrust in seconde, you may oppose it by forming the simple parade of semicircle. *See plate* 14.—And as he recovers, counter disengage, and deliver a thrust in octave. *See lesson* 6.

2d. On the engagement of carte, your adversary counter disengages and thrusts octave, which oppose by the parade of circle, then deliver a thrust in low carte.

3d. On

3d. On the same engagement, if he counter disengages, you may drop first in semicircle, but missing his blade, instantly form your simple parade in octave, in order to baffle his counter disengagements. (*See plate* 12.)—then make a straight return of the thrust in octave.

4th. On the same engagement, counter disengage in semicircle, or to octave; he attempts to parry it, by following your blade with the parade of circle; then double and thrust octave.

5th On the same engagement, he counter disengages, follow his blade by the circle parade; if he attempts to double, stop him by forming the simple parade of octave. (*See plate* 12.) and return the thrust thereof.

6th. On the same engagement, he counter disengages; form the parades of semicircle and octave, which answers both movements; then, disengage over his arm,

arm, as if you intended to thruſt low carte; but deceive him by counter diſengaging and thruſting octave.

7th. On the engagement of tierce, if your adverſary thruſts octave or low carte, you may parry it with octave. (*See plate* 12.) Then counter diſengage, and deliver a thruſt in low carte.

8th. On the ſame engagement, he counter diſengages and thruſts low carte, which oppoſe by your counter parade in octave, and return the thruſt thereof.

9th. On the ſame engagement, he again counter diſengages and thruſts low carte, which you may baffle by firſt forming the ſimple parade of octave, then forming the parade of ſemicircle quickly after the other;—and as he recovers, counter diſengage and thruſt octave.

10th. On the ſame engagement, he counter diſengages, as if intending to thruſt low carte, follow his blade

blade by the counter parade in octave, he attempts to double or disengage again; but baffle him by forming your simple parade of semicircle; then as he recovers, disengage over the arm, and deliver the thrust in octave.

11th. On the same engagement, you may counter disengage, as if intending to thrust low carte, he follows your blade by the counter parade in octave; disengage again, and if you find that he will oppose it by semicircle, nimbly disengage the last time, and thrust octave.

12th. On the same engagement, he counter disengages;—answer both his movements by the simple parade of octave and semicircle; and if he attempts to make you lose the feel of his blade, by again counter disengaging, follow it by the counter parade of octave; then you may either return a straight thrust in octave, or counter disengage as he recovers, and deliver a thrust in low carte.

Remark.

Remark. The above are the most essential practical variations on the counter parades and counter disengagements of semicirle and octave, to be used in assaults, when your adversary uses his low parades.

LESSON XI.

Of the practical Variations on the Counter Parades and Thrusts of Prime and Seconde.

BRANCH first. On the engagement of tierce, advance within measure, forcing upon your adversary's blade,—if he betakes himself to the simple parade

The Parade of Semicircle against the Thrust of Seconde.

parade of prime, counter difengage and thruft feconde. *See leffon* 7.

2d. On the fame engagement, he advances, forces, and counter difengages as above; but baffle his thruft in feconde, by the counter parade in prime, (*See leffon* 4.) and return the thruft thereof.

3d. On the fame engagement, he again counter difengages as aforefaid;—anfwer both his movements, by firft dropping in prime, then in feconde, which will parry his counter difengagement; then as he recovers, you may either thruft feconde, or counter difengage and thruft prime.

4th. On the fame engagement, he counter difengages, follow his blade by the counter parade in prime; if he attempts to double or difengage again, ftop him, by forming your fimple parade of feconde.

5th. On

5th. On the engagement of carte, counter difengage, when your adverfary drops in feconde, and thruft prime. *See leffon* 7.

6th. On the fame engagement, he counter difengages when you drop to feconde; oppofe it by forming your counter parade of feconde, then return a ftraight thruft in feconde. Or, if on the fame engagement he makes a ftraight thruft in feconde, you may parry it with femicircle, (*See plate* 14.) and return low carte thruft.

7th. On the fame engagement, he counter difengages, anfwer his movements, by forming the fimple parades of feconde and prime, then counter difengage as he recovers, and deliver a thruft in feconde.

8th. On the fame engagement, counter difengage when he drops to feconde; but if he follows your blade clofely, by the counter parade of feconde, then double and thruft feconde.

9th. On

9th. On the same engagement, he counter disengages, follow his blade by the counter parade of seconde; if he attempts to double, baffle him, by forming your simple parade in prime.

10th. On the same engagement, he counter disengages and doubles, follow his blade closely, by forming or doubling the counter parade of seconde; then as he recovers, counter disengage and thrust prime, by making a full longe.

11th. On the same engagement, he counter disengages, answer his movements by the simple parades of seconde and prime; he causes you to lose his blade by disengaging again, follow it by the counter in prime.— Or in place of this counter parade, form your simple parade of seconde, and deliver a thrust in return.

12th. On the same engagement, force upon your adversary's blade; if he does not disengage, he will naturally oppose it a little; then drop your point under his wrist, and make a feint, as if you intended to thrust seconde; if he comes to parry it with the simple parade of seconde, immediately counter disengage, and deliver your thrust in prime.

LESSON XII.

Of the different Feints.

FEINTS are used in attacks, in order to oblige your adversary, to give you some openings, either one way or other. The simple feints *une deux*, or *one, two*, is performed by two separate disengagements, either on the engagement of carte or tierce, when your adversary throws his simple parades. If engaged in carte, disengage closely to tierce, then quickly disengage back to carte, delivering the thrust thereof. *See part 1. lesson 10.*

On the engagement of tierce, disengage first to carte, then disengage back to tierce, delivering the thrust of carte over the arm.

Feint flanconnade, carte infide, is performed on the engagament of carte, by binding your adverfary's blade a little, as if you intended to thruft flanconnade; but deceive him, by thrufting carte infide. You may alfo mark this feint, and deliver a thruft over the arm by difengaging.

Feint feconde, carte over the arm, is performed when engaged in tierce, by dropping your point and reverfing the nails, as if you meant to thruft feconde; then quickly reverfe them upwards, and deliver the thruft of carte over the arm. On the fame engagement, you may mark feint feconde, and thruft carte infide, if there is an opening.

Feints *une-deux-trois*, or *one, two, three*, are performed by three feparate difengagements, either from the engagement of carte or tierce. On the engagement of carte, mark feint one two, as above; finding your adverfary comes to form his fimple parade of carte; then nimbly mark your third difengagement, by thrufting thrusting carte over the arm. On the engagement of tierce, disengage three times, and deliver your thrust in carte inside. *See practical variations on feints, lesson* 16.

Please to observe, that these disengagements should be performed nimbly by the motion of the wrist, holding the foil flexible in your hand. *See lesson* 9. *part* 1.

LES-

LESSON XIII.

Of the Cuts over the Point, thrust of the Wrist on recovering, Return of the Wrist, and Return on the Extension, &c.

CUT over the point is performed, when you perceive that your adversary holds his hand low, and his point raised upon guard. To perform it from carte to tierce, your foil should be easy in your hand, and the wrist flexible; then raise your point quickly with the upward motion of your wrist fairly over your adversary's point, without moving your arm from the line of direction; at the same time, forming your extension, deliver your thrust of carte over the arm. If he comes to parry with simple tierce, you

you may cut over the point again to carte, and deliver the thrust of carte inside.

In the same manner, you may execute cuts over the point, from the engagement of tierce, when your adversary holds his point high. If there is an opportunity of executing these cuts over the point, they answer the purpose of disengagements, and seem more perplexing to your adversary.

The thrust of the wrist is performed, when you perceive your adversary slow in making a return, after you have longed with a thrust. It may in this case be a very safe and succesful thrust, if delivered with vivacity as you recover.—To perform it on the engagement of carte, suppose you thrust carte over the arm, which your adversary naturally parries with simple tierce. Lean with some degree of force upon his blade, and as you recover to guard, deliver him a thrust with the wrist in seconde.

On the same engagement, disengage to carte over the arm; if he parries it with semicircle, and is slow in

making

making a return; you may disengage over his arm, and deliver him a thrust with the wrist as you recover.

In the same manner, you may perform the thrust of the wrist from the engagement of tierce, by disengaging and thrusting carte inside, which he parries, by the simple parade of carte; then force a little upon his blade, and deliver him a thrust with the wrist in low carte, as you recover.

The return of the wrist, also the return on the extension, is performed after your adversary makes a full longe with a thrust, which you must make sure to parry so powerfully, as to throw his arm out of the line of direction; then with all possible quickness extend your arm, and deliver him a straight thrust in return before he has time to recover. If the extension of the arm is not within reach, form your compleat extension of the leg and arm. (*See plate* 8.)

LESSON XIV.

Of the Appels or Beats with the Foot, Beats on the Blade, and Glizades.

THIS lesson, with the practical variations thereon, contains without doubt, the most essential movements in fencing, after having made the necessary progress in all the foregoing lessons; because these appels, beats, and glizades tend to plant you firm upon guard, to embarrass your adversary, and causes him to give you some openings, in order to facilitate your designs; and they may be performed previous to simple thrusts, feints, or counter disengagements, &c.—An appel or beat with the foot is performed either on the engagement of carte or tierce, within or without measure, by suddenly raising and letting fall the right foot, with a beat on the same spot; taking care to balance your body, and keep a good position on guard.

The beat on the blade is performed by abruptly touching your adversary's blade, so as to startle him, and get openings to thrust.—If he resists the beat, instantaneously disengage, and thrust home. If he comes to use a simple parade, mark feint one, two; or if he uses a counter parade, counter disengage or double.

Glizades are performed, by slightly gliding your blade along your adversary's, at the same time forming either the extension of the arm, or the compleat extension, managing and restraining your body, so as to be aware of his thrusts, and to make sure of your own.

If you are engaged in carte out of measure, a quick advance, with a glizade, must infallibly give you some openings, either to mark feints or otherwise.—*See practical variations, lesson* 19.

LES-

LESSON XV.

Of the Time Thrust, and practical Variations thereon.

THIS thrust is performed by instantaneously seizing the time, when you find that your adversary is aukward and dilatory in his guards, parades, feints, and thrusts. Formerly this thrust was looked upon as hazardous to attempt in serious affairs, and only used as an ornamental thrust in the exercise of lessons with foils: but now, it is universally introduced into accademies or schools for fencing; and practised in common with the other useful thrusts.

I must confess, that to execute this thrust with nicety, requires a quick eye, a susceptible hand, a volatile movement, and juſt poſition. But when theſe requiſites are attained or attended to, there can be no more hazard or difficulty in putting this excellent thruſt in certain execution, than any other uſed in fencing.

If in attempting to deliver this thruſt, when an opportunity offers, you cover yourſelf well, by forming a gradual and ſtrong oppoſition to your adverſary's blade; you can be in no danger of expoſing yourſelf to an interchanged thruſt, (that is, a thruſt at the ſame moment from your adverſary). It is from the erroneous principles generally taught by maſters, that danger may ſeem to ariſe in executing the time thruſt, and not from the thruſt itſelf, which is founded upon the moſt eaſy and ſimple principles in nature, and is liable to many practical variations; the moſt uſeful are as follows;

Branch 1ſt. On the engagement of carte, your adverſary diſengages to tierce, that inſtant quickly diſengage alſo contrarily, (that is to carte,) and puſh home. (*See plate* 15.)

2d. On

Time thrust upon your Adversary's Disengaging to Tierce.

2d. On the engagement of tierce, he difengages to carte, then difengage contrarily, and thruft home carte over the arm.

3d. On the engagement of carte, when you find that your adverfary holds his hand too low upon guard, and deviates from the guard rules; feize the opening by pufhing carte ftraight home.

4th. On the engagement of tierce, having the like opportunity; deliver the thruft of carte over the arm ftraight home.

5th. On the engagement of carte, if your adverfary feints one, two, and makes his difengagements wide; feize the time, and pufh ftraight home. This may be alfo executed when on the engagement of tierce.

6th. On the engagement of carte, he difengages, and attempts to difarm you, by beating your blade in tierce, then difengage contrarily, and deliver a thruft in carte.

7th. On

7th. On the same engagement, if your adversary leans heavy, and presses upon your blade, instantly disengage, and deliver him a thrust in carte over the arm; adverting to cover yourself well.

8th. On the same engagement, retreat; and if your adversary upon advancing should disengage, and force upon your blade; disengage also, and push carte inside.

9th. On the same engagement, disengage, as if going to push carte over the arm; your adversary opposes it by his counter parade in carte, making a wide circle, then push carte straight home; taking care to form a powerful opposition against your adversary's blade.

10th. On the engagement of tierce; if upon your disengaging he should form his counter parade in tierce, then push carte over the arm.

11th. On the engagement of carte, he drops his point under your wrist, and thrusts low carte; oppose it by forming your opposition strongly in octave; and at the same time yielding forward on your extension; you will not only parry his thrust, but also touch him. *See plate* 8.

N. B. This may be termed *a return on the extension* after the parade of octave. Or with greater propriety, it may be termed *a time thrust on the extension*, as it almost comprehends the same moment of time.

12th. On the engagement of carte, he makes the movement of a cut over your point; upon this motion nimbly disengage contrarily; that is, to carte inside, and deliver him the thrust thereof. Or, on this engagement, you may, upon his motion to cut over the point, deliver the time thrust in carte over the arm. (*See plate* 17.)

L E S-

LESSON XVI.

Of the practical Variations on the different Feints.

BRANCH first. On the engagement of carte, mark feint one, two, thrust carte inside, *See lesson* 12.

2d. On the engagement of tierce, mark feint one, two, and thrust carte over the arm.

3d. On the engagement of carte, mark a feint over the arm, and thrust low carte.

4th. On the same engagement, mark feint over the arm, reverse the wrist, and thrust seconde.

5th. On

5th. On the same engagement, mark the feint in flanconnade, and thrust carte inside.

6th. On the same engagement, mark feint, flanconnade, disengage; and thrust carte over the arm.

7th. On the same engagement, mark feint one two; and thrust flanconnade.

8th. On the engagement of tierce, mark feint seconde, reverse the wrist, and thrust carte over the arm.

9th. On the same engagement, mark feint seconde, thrust carte inside.

10th. On the engagement of carte, in attempting the feints one, two, he baffles it by his counterparade in carte, then counter disengage, and deliver the thrust of carte over the arm.

11th. On the same engagement, he baffles your feint, by forming semicircle, then counter disengage, and deliver a thrust in octave.

12th. On the engagement of tierce, he baffles your feints one two, by his counter parade of tierce, then nimbly counter disengage, and thrust carte inside.

13th. on the same engagement, in attempting feint one two, he baffles you, by his parade in octave, then counter disengage, and thrust low carte.

14th. On the engagement of carte, if your adversary is accustomed to form his simple parades; you may mark feints one, two, three, by three separate disengagements, and thrust carte over the arm. (*See lesson* 12.)

15th. On the engegement of tierce, mark feints one, two, three, and deliver your thrust of carte inside.

16th. On

16th. On the engagement of carte, mark feints one, two, three, and deliver your thrust in octave, in place of carte over the arm.

17th. On the engagement of tierce, mark feints one, two, three, and deliver your thrust in low carte.

18th. On the engagement of carte, mark feint over the arm, then mark feint seconde; if he comes to parry it with semicircle, counter disengage, and thrust seconde.

LESSON XVII.

Of the practical Variations on the Cuts over the Point, &c.

BRANCH first. On the engagement of carte, suppose your adversary holds his guard low, and his point high;—make a cut over the point, forming your extension, and thrust carte over the arm. *See lesson* 13.

2d. On the engagement of carte, cut over the point; if he uses a simple parade, disengage, and thrust carte inside.

3d. On the same engagement, cut over the point twice, and thrust carte inside.

4th. On the engagement of tierce, your adverſary holds his hand low, and point high, make a cut over the point, and thruſt carte inſide.

5th. On the ſame engagement, cut over the point twice, and deliver the thruſt of carte over the arm.

6th. On the ſame engagement, cut over the point twice, then diſengage and thruſt carte inſide.

7th. On the engagement of carte, cut over the point, mark feints one, two, and thruſt carte over the arm.

8th. On the engagement of tierce, cut over the point, then mark feints one, two, and thruſt carte inſide.

9th. On the engagement of carte, cut over the point, if your adverſary takes his counter parade in carte, inſtantly counter diſengage, and thruſt carte over the arm.

10th. On

10th. On the engagement of tierce, cut over the point; if he ufes his counter parade in tierce, counter difengage, and thruft carte infide.

11th. On the engagement of carte, cut over the point; if he oppofes it with a fimple parade, difengage under his wrift, and thruft octave.

12th. On the engagement of tierce, cut over the point; if he oppofes it with fimple carte, drop your point under his wrift, and thruft low carte.

LESSON XVIII.

Of the practical Variations on the Thrust of the Wrist, and Thrust of Extension.

BRANCH first. On the engagement of carte, disengage to tierce, and thrust carte over the arm; if your adversary forms his simple parade in tierce, and is slow in making a return, deliver him a thrust with the wrist in seconde as you recover. *(See lesson 13.)*

2d. On the engagement of tierce, disengage and thrust carte; if he parries it with simple carte, and is slow in making a return, deliver him a thrust with the wrist in low carte, as you recover.

3d. On the engagement of carte, disengage and thrust carte over the arm; if he parries it with semicircle, and is slow in making a return, disengage over his arm as you recover, and deliver him a thrust in octave.

4th. On the engagement of tierce, disengage and thrust carte inside, or low carte; if he parries it with octave, disengage over his arm as you recover, and deliver him a thrust in low carte.

5th. On the engagement of carte, disengage and thrust seconde; if he parries it with seconde, counter disengage as you recover, and thrust prime.

6th. On the engagement of tierce, force upon his blade, disengage and thrust low carte; he parries it with prime, *See plate* 10. and is slow in making a return; deliver the thrust in seconde with the wrist as you recover.

7th. On the engagement of carte, force upon his blade, in order to give him an opening; he disengages and delivers a thrust over the arm, which you oppose
justly

juftly and powerfully, by forming the fimple parade of tierce; then quickly extend your arm, and deliver him a ftraight thruft in tierce or in feconde before he can recover. (*See leffon* 13. concerning the return of the wrift.)

8th. On the engagement of tierce, force upon his blade, which will oblige him to thruft carte infide; throw it well off, by powerfully forming your parade in carte; then with the extenfion of the arm, deliver him a ftraight thruft in carte, before he has time to recover.

9th. On the engagement of carte, give him fome openings; if he marks the feints one, two, and thrufts, form your counter parade in carte; then deliver him a quick return with the wrift in low carte, by forming the compleat extenfion.

10th. On the engagement of tierce, in like manner give him fome openings; if he marks feints one, two, and

and thrusts, form your counter parade in tierce, and on the extenfion, deliver him a thruft in feconde.

11th. On the engagement of carte, if he executes low feints and thrufts, ufe the circle parade, and return a ftraight thruft on the extenfion before he recovers.

12th. On the engagement of tierce, if he feints and thrufts low; oppofe them by the fimple or counter parade in octave, forming well the oppofition, and directing the point to his body, which will at the fame time hit him. Or at any rate, you muft inevitably touch him by the extenfion, if your arm and parade is juftly directed and formed. (*See plate* 8.)

This is certainly the beft return in fencing, as I have formerly obferved.

LESSON XIX.

Of the practical Variations on Appels, Beats on the Blade, and Glizades.

BRANCH first. On the engagement of carte, make an appel, or beat with the right foot, at the the same time beating abruptly on your adversary's blade, which will give you an opening to thrust carte straight home.

2d. On the same engagement, make an appel, beat his blade, then disengage, and thrust carte over the arm.

3d. On the engagement of tierce, make an appel, beat his blade, and thruſt tierce or carte over the arm.

4th. On the ſame engagement, make an appel, beat his blade; then diſengage and deliver a thruſt in carte inſide.

5th. On the engagement of carte, make an appel, diſengage, and beat his blade in tierce; and if there is an opening in tierce, ſeize it, and deliver a ſtraight thruſt.

6th. On the ſame engagement, make an appel, diſengage to tierce, and beat his blade; then diſengage again, and thruſt carte inſide.

7th. On the engagement of tierce, make your appel, diſengage to carte by beating his blade, and thruſt carte inſide.

8th. On the engagement of carte, make your appel, mark the feints one, two, and thruſt carte inſide.

9th. On

9th. On the same engagement, disengage and beat his blade, then mark feints one, two, and thrust carte over the arm.

10th. On the engagement of carte, make a glizade along his blade, forming your extension; if he does not cover himself, deliver a straight thrust in carte.

11th. On the engagement of tierce, perform a glizade along his blade, with the extension; if he does not cover himself, deliver a straight thrust in carte over the arm.

12th. On rhe engagement of carte, make a glizade, drop your point, and deliver a thrust in low carte.

13th. On the engagement of tierce, perform a glizade, drop your point under his wrist, and deliver a thrust in octave.

14th. On the engagement of carte, make an appel and glizade; at the same time disengage to tierce, if he uses a counter parade, disengage again, and deliver the thrust over the arm.

15th. On the engagement of tierce, make an appel and glizade, disengage to carte inside, if he takes the counter parade in tierce, then disengage a second time, and thrust carte inside.

16th. On the engagement of carte, perform an appel and glizade, mark feints one, two, and thrust carte inside.

17th. On the same engagement, perform an appel and glizade, then mark feints one, two, and deliver your thrust in low carte.

18th. On the engagement of tierce, perform an appel and glizade, mark feints one, two, and thrust octave.

Remark.

Remark. Besides the above variations on appels and glizades the learner may execute the various movements in the different branches of *lessons* 16 *and* 17.—always beginning these movements with an appel and glizade, or with a glizade alone.

In order to facilitate your improvement, and for the more speedy attaining execution, together with justness in your parades, thrusts, and other movements; you should frequently exercise with a person who may have made similar progress, by executing against him all the feints, counter disengagements, and thrusts of the practical variations, while he is firmly planted upon guard defensively, making use of the various parades as occasion may require, or his judgment dictate.

In return, he may exercise these practical movements against you, while upon guard, endeavouring to oppose them by just and natural parades.—This must mutually improve,

improve, as there can be no dread of a return of any thruſt from each other*.

* The dotted ellipſes or ovals deſcribed in the mathematical illuſtrations of the counter parades, are to ſhow the perſpective view of the point's courſe in forming theſe parades.

PART

PART III.

OF

ASSAULTS AND ATTACKS IN GENERAL.

PART III.

OF

ASSAULTS AND ATTACKS IN GENERAL;

CONTAINING

Some useful Observations on the Time Thrust; the most advantageous Manner of Attacking an Adversary, either out of Measure, or in Measure. Also, Rules and Observations in single Combat with Swords; and the most eligible Method of Disarming an Adversary in fencing with a Foil; or, in serious Affairs, with a Sword.

AN ASSAULT with foils, is in imitation of a single combat with swords, where you execute against your adversary, all the feints, thrusts, and parades of the foregoing lessons,—endeavouring to embrace every advantage and opportunity to embarrass and deceive him, in order to render your thrusts and parades effectual.—But,

Previous to engaging in assaults, it is an established rule in academies, to make the following salute.

On the engagement of tierce, make two quick appels, or beats with your right foot; bring it close behind the left, near the buckle; raising and stretching your right arm, with the nails upwards, and the point of your foil dropp'd;—at the same time, take off your hat with a grace, and hold it in your left hand, stretched down near the flank; then, with a circular motion of the wrist, as if forming the counter in tierce, throw your left foot backwards, to the distance of your common guard, raising your left hand, make other two appels;—bring your left foot forward to the former position, that is, before the right, near the buckle; at the same time stretching your arm, with the nails upwards as before. And in that position, form

gracefully

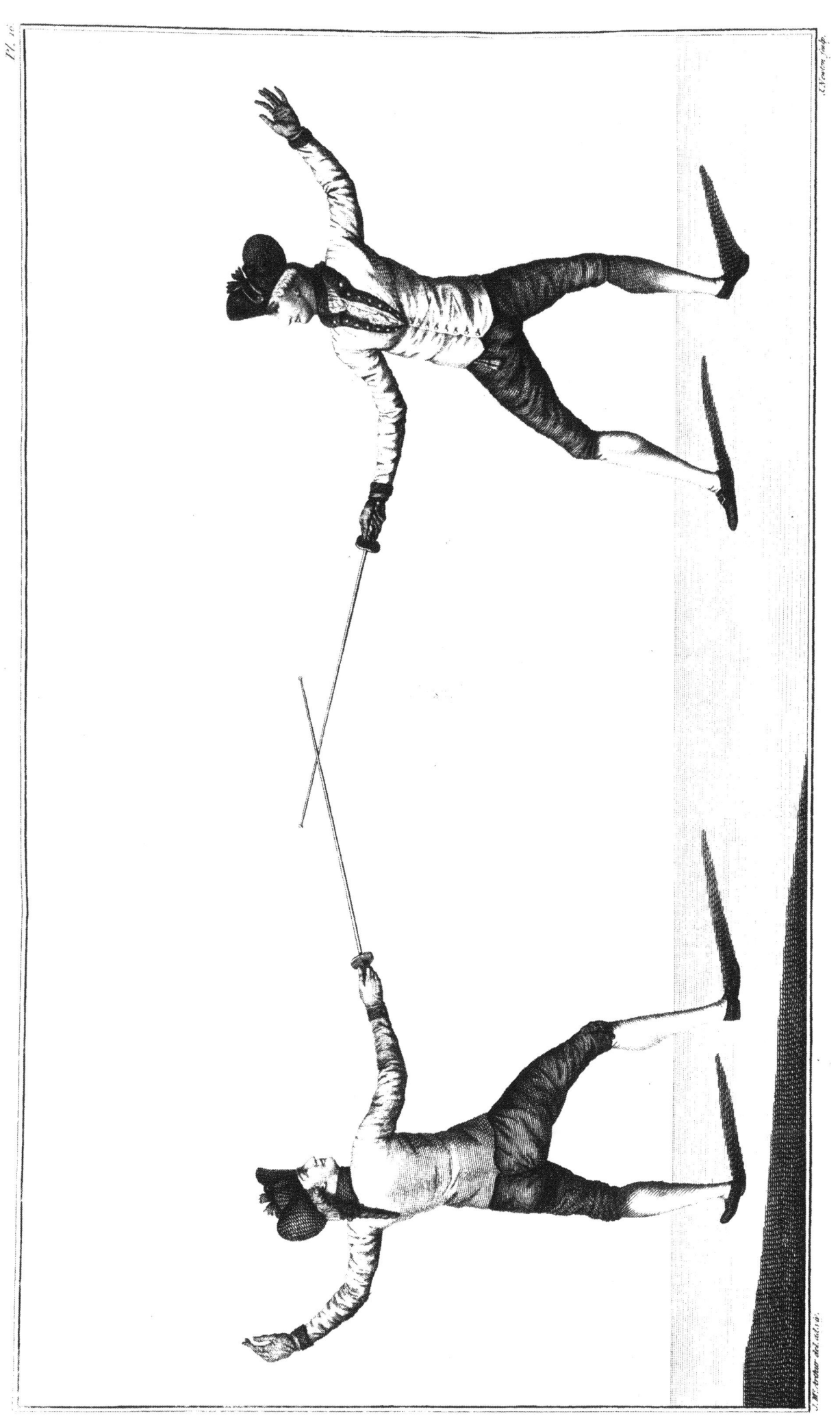

The Guards upon joining Blades for an Assault.

London, Publish'd Dec.r 1.1780 by J. Laws N.o 10 Strand.

gracefully the parade of carte and tierce; make a circular motion with the wrist, and advance your right foot with vivacity to your original guard, at the same time covering your head.

All the movements in this salute, should be performed in a more lively manner than those in the salute, previous to thrusting carte and tierce; (*See part* 2. *lesson* 1.) and please to observe, that these movements should keep exactly the same time with your adversary's.

When you first enter upon the assault, you may engage your adversary's blade out of measure in carte, as being easier than the other engagement for executing your different movements. (*See plate* 16.) Assume a bold air, and steady position. Steadily fix your eyes to those of your adversary, so that he may not penetrate into your designs, and withal advert to keep your proper distance and measure.

It is a moſt eſſential point in aſſaults, to know exactly the diſtance and meaſure; and for that purpoſe you muſt obſerve the height of your adverſary, length of the foil, &c. and make the neceſſary allowances accordingly.

Pleaſe to obſerve, never to fence in aſſaults with ſhort foils, but have them always of a proper length, which will enable you to keep a regular diſtance, and execute your movements with more juſtneſs and dexterity; beſides, it will in ſome degree prevent you from contracting the erroneous habits you might be liable to imbibe by fencing with ſhort foils.

If your adverſary is a tall perſon, it is prudent to engage out of meaſure, and allow him to make the firſt attack, that you may know the extent of his longe, &c.—When intending to attack him, you muſt execute your feints nimbly; advancing, in order to gain your meaſure, and deliver him the intended thruſt.

You should always indeed avoid making the first attack against any adversary, skilled or not, in fencing, let his stature be high or low; for you will find it more to your advantage, to act for some time at first on the defensive; always varying your parade, in order to embarrass him, and put him to a stand how to act. By these means, you will at once perceive his favourite feints and thrusts, and his general method of attacking.

On the engagement of carte, if your adversary advances to gain his measure, you may give him an opening to thrust carte over the arm, by forcing a little upon his blade, which perhaps will oblige him to disengage and thrust carte over the arm; parry it strongly with simple tierce, and deliver in return, either the thrust of tierce, or thrust of seconde.

On the same engagement, if he attacks you, by performing feints one, two, or feints one, two, three, use your counter parade in carte, or you may baffle his feints by the

simple

simple parade of semicircle. If he counter disengages when you form semicircle, I would advise you, immediately to take octave parade, and return the thrust thereof. This parade, on the engagement of carte, I think preferable to the circle parade in baffling a counter disengagement, particularly when your adversary is within measure; for, unless you have made great progress in fencing, it is almost impracticable to follow his blade by the circle parade, so as to parry his counter disengagement, if executed quickly.

On the same engagement, if he makes frequent disengagements with a view to get openings, and know the parades you seem most inclinable to use, you should seldom or never answer them, by forming any parade; but, stand firm and easy upon guard, and do not appear hurried or embarrassed by any small feints or disengagements he may perform. If you do answer his feints, beats, and disengagements, let it be in such manner, that he cannot possibly judge what parade you seem inclinable to prefer. This you may effect, by
alternately

alternately changing your parades; sometimes using simple tierce and carte; other times using the counter parade in carte, semicircle, &c.

If your adversary makes frequent practice of disengaging, beating your blade, and otherwise embarrassing you, with a view to get openings, you may seize the time, and deliver a quick thrust, taking care to cover yourself well, by forming a good opposition against his blade. This is called the time thrust; and if dexterously executed, must be looked upon as one of the finest thrusts in fencing, (*See part* 2. *lesson* 15.) To perform it with any degree of nicety, does not depend upon the eye alone, but mostly upon a kind of feeling or susceptibility that the hand must necessarily have; which practice, and your own judgment alone, will assist you in, or cause you to imbibe; for there can be no proper rules laid down for attaining this feeling, so necessary in fencing, especially in executing the time thrust.

There may be various occasions for performing the time thrust; *(See practical variations, part 2. lesson 15.)* but the most adventageous I have experienced on the engagement of carte, is when your adversary disengages with a view to beat your blade in tierce; then instantaneously feeling the motion of his disengagement, disengage contrarily, and quickly deliver a thrust carte inside, forming a good opposition, in order to avoid an interchanged thrust. In the same manner, if his feints are executed wide, you may also seize the time, and push straight home.

Another favourable occasion for performing this thrust on the same engagement, is, when your adversary, out of measure, advances to gain it by disengaging; seize the time, and thrust straight carte over the arm; or you may counter disengage, and thrust carte inside.

Again, on the same engagement, by way of snare, hold your point higher than usual; if he attempts to make a cut over the point, that instant feeling the motion,

Time thrust in Carte upon an Adversary's motion to cut over the Point.

London, Publish'd Dec.r.1.1780 by J.Lavers N.o.30. Strand.

motion, disengage contrarily, and thrust carte inside; or, you may, in preference to this, deliver a straight thrust in carte over the arm. (*See plate* 17.)

The time thrust may be performed with safety on the extension, if your adversary makes a full longe, and is neither sure of his measure, nor covered on his longe.—For example, on the engagement of carte, he disengages over the arm, form your parade of semicircle, he will naturally counter disengage, in order to thrust octave; then instantaneously form your opposition strongly in octave; yield forward on the extension, and fix your point well towards his flank. This, if justly executed, seldom fails in parrying your adversary's thrust, and touching him at the same moment. (*See plate* 8. *also lesson* 7. *part* 1. *and lesson* 15. *part* 2.)

The time thrust is liable to similar variations on the engagement of tierce; of which I shall say a little, when I come to treat of that engagement in assaults.

When you engage in the assault, be not too eager in making your thrusts or returns; as by an over eagerness, young learners for the most part contract a habit of returning their thrusts, by crooking the arm, which is quite erroneous. Always observe to form your parades justly, and accustom yourself at first, to make straight returns without disengaging. If your parade is well formed, you must undoubtedly make a good straight thrust in return. If you intend to return a thrust by disengaging, you should perform it the moment your adversary is recovering, it must proceed nimbly from the motion of the wrist, and not by crooking the arm. (*See lesson* 9. *part* 1.) concerning disengagements.

The distance of your guard should never exceed two measured feet; as by a wide guard, you keep your adversary at too great distance, and have not that necessary command of throwing your body back far enough when he advances, and makes a full longe. Neither can you retreat, or make returns with necessary quickness.

quickness. And besides, the lower part of your body is more exposed than it would be on a proper medium guard.

If you engage the blade in carte, cover your inside a little, so as to have nothing to fear from a straight thrust on that engagement. In like manner, if you are engaged in tierce, cover your outside, to prevent straight thrusts on that engagement.

If on the engagement of carte you are inclined to attack your adversary, disengage dexterously outside and inside, by forming your extension, as if intending to thrust. If it does not give you openings, you may expect to discover the parades he will use. If he uses his simple parades, you will easily deceive him, by marking feints one, two, or feints one, two, three. But if your adversary is skilful, and uses his counter parades variously; you must endeavour to embarrass him by appels, extensions, glizades, beatings of the blade, counter disengagements, &c. (*See practical lessons in part* 2.)

The

The most adventageous method of attacking such an adversary on the engagement of carte, I shall briefly describe in the few following examples.

1st. On the engagement of carte, being within measure, perform an appel and glizade. If he resists your glizade, by forcing on the blade, holding at the same time his wrist low and point high, make a nimble cut over the point, which he will naturally come to parry with simple tierce; then quickly disengage and deliver the thrust of carte inside.

2d. On the same engagement, if you are out of measure, make a quick and regular advance in order to gain it; at same time extending your arm, and forming a glizade along your adversary's blade; he will perhaps, resist it, by leaning on your blade; then disengage to carte over the arm, forming your compleat extension; if he uses the simple parade in tierce, disengage and thrust carte inside;—but if he uses the counter parade in carte, counter disengage and deliver your thrust.

3d. On

3d. On the other engagement, if out of measure, advance in like manner with a glizade; make an appel, and quickly disengage under his wrist, and deliver him a quick thrust in low carte. If he is in time to parry this thrust with semicircle, you must recover quickly, fixing your point well to his body, and forming the parade of semicircle, octave, or the counter in carte, just according as he thrusts in return; but if he is slow in making a return, you may safely, on recovering, deliver him a thrust of the wrist.

4th. On the same engagement, if you are within measure, make an appel and glizade, drop to low carte, and form your extension; if your adversary comes to parry it with semicircle, counter disengage, and deliver a thrust in octave; if he comes to follow your blade with the circle parade, you may double, and then thrust octave.

N. B. These two examples may be performed advantageously against an adversary that is very tall in statute.

5th. On

5th. On the same engagement, having performed a glizade, and marked a feint in low carte; if you find your adversary will answer the movement of your counter disengagement, by first forming semicircle, then octave; in place of fully counter disengaging to octave, you should only half disengage; that is, to the height of his arm; lose a moment of time, till he forms the parade of octave; then deliver your thrust straight carte inside.

This example is very deceiving, when your adversary frequently uses the simple parades of semicircle and octave alternately.

6th. On the same engagement, perform a glizade, and disengage to carte over the arm, raising your hand, and extending the arm; if he takes his counter parade, counter disengage, or double, or if he attempts to throw it off by the simple parade of tierce; you may in either cases deceive him, and make your thrust effectual, by dropping your point, and thrusting to his belly or flank, taking always particular care to

cover

cover yourself, by making a good opposition on your thrusts.—This last example is also very deceiving, when your adversary forms his high parades as above; and is an advantageous attack against an adversary of a tall stature.

It would render this treatise too tedious to describe and lay down the various methods of attacking your adversary on the engagement of carte. The six preceeding examples, if well executed, I flatter myself, will, will suffice, equally as well as six hundred. I have, from experience, found the movements contained in these examples, to be the most eligible manner of attacking an adversary on this engagement, and the surest method of rendering your intended thrusts effectual. The learner may have recourse to the various practical lessons in *part* 2. which will further assist his taste and judgment in varying his mode of attacking on this engagement.

When you engage your adverfary's blade in tierce, I would alfo advife you to bear his firft attacks, acting defenfively for fome time, in order that you may difcover what feints or thrufts he inclines to ufe on that engagement. The counter parade in tierce, fimple octave, and the counter in octave, will parry almoft every feint and thruft that he can poffibly make. On this engagement, you may alternately perform thefe parades, in order to baffle his difengagements; vary them occafionally with the parades of feconde and femicircle, which will prevent him from knowing what parade you feem moft inclinable to ufe againft his intended thrufts.

If a good fencer feems to prefer one parade before another, he may be eafily deceived, and frequently touched by a perfon not near fo fkilful as himfelf. Therefore, it is affuredly the beft way for a learner to put in practice all the parades, changing them every moment, as occafion requires. He fhould fly from the high to the low parades, and *vice verfa*, fo that in the end, he will find it no difficult matter to parry every feint and thruft.

For

For example; on the engagement of tierce, your adverſary diſengages to carte, follow his blade by the counter parade of tierce; he, in order to deceive you, drops his point, and thruſts octave or low carte; ſo that dropping to the parade of ſemicircle and octave, the moment you have miſſed his blade in the counter parade of tierce, will certainly be in time to parry his thruſt. Hence you ſhould avoid making your parades too ſtrong or wide, in caſe of miſſing his blade, that you may the more eaſily go from the upper to the lower parades.

Again, on the ſame engagement, he makes a feint in octave, with a view to get an opening in carte; not knowing his deſign, form your parade in octave; and the moment you loſe his blade, bring your hand round to the ſimple parade of carte, which will intercept his blade in the counter diſengagement or intended thruſt of carte. You will find it exceedingly uſeful, to go from the parade of octave to carte; as it baffles a variety of feints and thruſts, that may be attempted on this engagement.

If your adversary advances within his measure, and forces in a straight thrust, carte over the arm, or in tierce, then raise and bend your arm, forming the parade of prime; (*See plate* 18.) and quickly return a straight thrust in prime before he recovers. Or, if you have not opening sufficient, disengage over his arm, and deliver your thrust in seconde.

On the same engagement, if your adversary attacks you by longeing when he is out of measure, you may lay a snare to touch him the moment he makes the longe.—For example, I shall suppose he intends to thrust, either octave or low carte, by feints or counter disengagements; then speedily perform your counter parade in octave, forming your extension, and powerfully opposing his blade; so that if your point is steadily fixed towards his flank, it will touch him on his longe. You may deceive him in this manner, even though he should attack you in proper measure, by retreating a step backwards out of measure, while he counter disengages and thrusts; at the same time forming your counter parade

in

The Parade of Prime against the force in Tierce or Thrust of Carte over the Arm.

London, Published Dec.r 1.5. 1780 by J. Leaves N°74 Strand.

in octave and extenfion as aforefaid. This is a kind of time thruft on the extenfion, and may be performed with fafety, when attacked out of meafure on the engagement of tierce.

On the fame engagement, if your adverfary makes his feints or difengages wide; you may feize the time, and deliver him a ftraight thruft, always taking care to be well covered when you longe.

On the fame engagement, in order to deceive your adverfary, retreat a ftep backwards, if he advances to gain his meafure; by difengaging to carte, inftantaneoufly difengage contrarily, and deliver the time thruft of carte over the arm.

On the fame engagement, if your adverfary forces or beats your blade, keeping his point raifed, immediately cut over the point to carte and thruft; if you find he will parry it with fimple carte, cut over the point and difengage; or if he ufes his counter parade in

tierce.

tierce, you muft counter difengage, and deliver your thruft.

Pleafe to obferve, never to extend yourfelf too far on the longe, as it impedes your recovering to guard with neceffary quicknefs.—Always endeavour to recover quickly, and with as much eafe as poffible, fixing your point to your adverfary's body; and forming the moft natural parade, in cafe he fhould make a quick return.

If engaged with an adverfary of a fhort ftature, I would advife you to attack him on the engagement of tierce, as being more advantageous for a number of feints and thrufts, than the engagement of carte.—Particularly for feint feconde, carte over the arm, &c.

It is alfo, in my opinion, the moft eligible engagement, for a fkillful fencer, who can execute the counter parades in tierce and octave with facility.—As the thrufts made in return after forming thefe parades juftly,
muft

muſt be effectual.—Beſides, it is the ſafeſt engagement for beating your adverſary's blade; ſo as to cauſe a diſarm, or at leaſt ſome openings.

The moſt advantageous manner which I have experienced, in attacking any adverſary on this engagement, I ſhall lay down in the few following examples; and the learner's judgement may improve thereon, or make additional variations thereto, as in the different practical leſſons.

1ſt. On the engagement of tierce, being out of meaſure, advance quickly, forming a glizade along your adverſary's blade; if that does not give you ſufficient opening, make an appel, and repeat the glizade, then diſengage to carte inſide; but if he comes to parry it with ſimple carte, diſengage again, and thruſt carte over the arm: if he comes to parry it with the counter in tierce; counter diſengage, and thruſt carte inſide; but if he comes to take the ſimple parade in carte against your counter disengagement, you should deceive him by thrusting carte over the arm.

On the same engagement, mark feint seconde, and deliver a thrust over your adversary's arm; or you may make a glizade along his blade; at the same time forming your extension, then quickly deliver him a thrust in octave; or you may deliver the thrust in seconde, by reversing the wrist; but if you find he will oppose it timeously, with the parade in octave or semicircle; you must carefully manage and restrain your body; deliver him a thrust in the first opening you can procure, by counter disengaging, or marking feints.

3d. On the same engagement, if within measure, make an appel and glizade, and disengage to carte, raising well your arm, as if intending to thrust to your adversary's breast. If he takes the simple parade of carte, or the counter in tierce; quickly drop your point under his wrist, and deliver him a thrust in low carte or octave.

You may occasionally vary the manner of executing this thrust, by counter disengaging or doubling, when he uses his counter parade; then suddenly drop your point, and thrust low carte or octave. In order to be aware of the above deception, if attempted by your adversary, you must the moment you lose sight of the blade in the upper parades, follow it by forming the lower ones. The above example will explain the utility of changing from the high to the low parades.

4th. On the same engagement, if you find your adversary inclinable to form his simple parades of octave and semicircle, without ever using a counter parade, you may sometimes deceive him in the following manner.—Mark a feint in seconde, which he will naturally offer to parry by simple octave or seconde; then mark another feint, as if you intended to thrust in low carte. But, in place of disengaging compleatly, you should only half disengage; that is, to the height of his wrist; then suddenly reverse your movement, and thrust

thrust seconde or octave, while he is forming his parade of semicircle, or any other simple parade to secure his inside. On the engagement of carte, I have described an example similar to the above.

On the engagement of tierce, you may execute a variety of other movements besides the above, by appels, and abrupt beats on your adversary's blade. *See practical variations, part 2.*

Notwithstanding all the variations that the art of fencing is susceptible of; yet it is confined to very few in the real execution of it, in serious affairs. Every one skilled in the art, always adopts some favourite parades, feints, and movements, which he naturally adheres to, and has a natural biafs to put in execution upon any emergency.

And though the custom of deciding points of honour by the sword, is not so frequent in this country, as in most foreign parts; yet noblemen, men of fashion, soldiers, and

and travellers of whatever degree or denomination, find manifold advantages from the cultivation and acqusition of this art, particularly in foreign countries, where the horrid practices of assassinations are frequently committed. Under a predicament of this nature, you must, in self defence, have recourse to the sensibility or feeling of your hand in all your movements, as being the only safe-guard in the dark.

I shall therefore mention a few of the most material rules and observations that have occurred to me on this subject, either when assaulted in a clandestine manner at night, or when engaged in single combat with any adversary. In support of these observations, I have at different times consulted the opinion of masters and foreigners skilled in the art; who have had their knowledge and judgement on these points, founded on long experience, often put to the test.

First then, when you are assaulted in the dark, and have time to draw your sword in defence; throw yourself on a wide guard, having your point well directed to your adverfary's breaft. By affuming a fierce and wide guard, he will think you are quite clofe upon him, and endeavour to feel his weapon, that you may engage it in carte or tierce. Having felt his blade, never quite it, but keep conftantly following any feints or difengagements he may attempt, by forming your counter parade of carte and tierce, femicircle, and octave, alternately ufing them, according to the fide engaged upon.

For example; if you feel his blade in carte, gently prefs upon it, that your hand may be the more fufceptible of his motions to difengage; and the inftant you feel the motion, follow him by the counter parade of carte. If you do not feel his blade with that parade, it muft be prefumed, that he has dropped his point under your arm. Therefore, in order to be aware of his thrufting low; after you have formed the counter parade of carte, inftantly form the fimple or counter parades of octave; and by bringing your hand with a

circular

circular movement to guard, you will always bring his blade to its former position.

Thefe two counter parades will baffle every feint and defign that he may attempt to execute againſt you on this engagement. They ſhould be executed with that dexterity, ſo as to ſeem a continuation of one parade; indeed, the courſes of the circles formed by each are the ſame; only, with this difference, the point is dropped, and wriſt bended, in forming the counter parade of octave.

If you ſhould feel your adverſary's blade on the engagement of tierce; the rules to be obſerved in ſelf-defence are nearly ſimilar to thoſe on the other engagement.

For example; preſs gently on his blade in tierce, and when you feel the motion of his diſengagement, quickly form your counter parade of tierce and parade of ſemicircle, (or circle, if neceſſary) bringing his blade

always

always round to the original position. If you happen to feel the blade with the counter parade of tierce only; it is very apt to cause a disarm, by the abrupt continuation of the two parades. These, if quickly executed, will also defend you from every feint or thrust that he may attempt against you on this engagement.

In executing these parades, the body should be well thrown back, and poised upon your left leg. If there is a space of ground to retreat, so much the better; but beware of the ruggedness of the ground, by raising your feet higher than common in retreating.

If the scene of action should be confined, and your adversary pressing vigorously upon you, with your back forced up to a wall, or any other corner; I would recommend you to make use of your simple parades of *seconde and prime* alternately; and when you have parried any of his thrusts forcibly with either of these parades; plunge one in return towards his flank or
belly,

belly, with the extenfion of the arm, making the oppofition correfpond with your parade.

For the more fpeedy attaining that degree of feeling neceffary, in the execution of the above ufeful parades; I would recommend fuch learners as have made fufficient progrefs in fencing, to exercife frequently thefe parades blindfolded in the field, or on any other rugged piece of ground, while another fcholar takes his proper diftance, and ufes every feint and ftratagem to deceive him.

The fmall fword in the hand of a fkilful fencer, has upon trial been found to prevail over an adverfary armed with a broad fword, cutlafs, or fcymitar, &c.—For, while he is raifing his hand to make a cut or blow at you, he is that moment liable to be run through the body, by a quick ftraight time thruft. In like manner, you may always prevail over an adverfary armed with a loaded piftol, provided it is prefented to you at fwords length, and the opportunity offers of joining your blade
thereto.

thereto. For if he offers to shift sides to level his aim, you can always prevent him with a counter parade, so that by keeping your blade joined to his pistol, and feeling his movements, you are covered securely from his fire. But if he should retreat, with a view to disengage his pistol from your blade, you must advance quickly towards him, endeavouring to keep the feel of his pistol, and deliver him a quick time thrust home. This is a hazardous attack for both parties; but the chance is as two to one in your favour.

Should necessity, or the punctillios of honour urge you to the field, to meet another in single combat, and that small sword should be the decisive weapons made choice of; you will find, perhaps, more difficulties than you are at first aware of.

For though your judgment and skill in fencing may be confessedly superior in every respect to an adversary, when engaged with foils on the *plastroon*, yet the erroneous habits he may imbibe or fall into, by an over

eagerness

eagerness in serious affairs, such as delivering thrusts with a crooked arm, forcibly beating down your guards, and frequently delivering random thrusts without being covered, may be the very cause of his prevailing over you: hence arise many fatal mistakes to skilful fencers, in serious affairs, who, too confident of their superiority over an adversary, and not aware of the thrusts of chance that he may deliver, often fall a victim to inferior skill. Many instances of this nature are daily exhibited on the Continent, where duelling in this manner so much prevails.

In order to be aware of an adversary, that delivers his thrusts furiously and with a crooked arm, you must retreat, forming the counter parades of carte and simple octave; and if he should continue eagerly advancing upon you, make a quick return on the extension, after you catch him with the parade of octave.

If an adversary should attack you with his left hand, always endeavour to engage him in carte, that will be, on his outside; and it will give you every advantage over him that he can poffibly have over you, particularly in attempts to difarm.

In ferious affairs few variations are practicable either on the parades, feints or thrufts. Every learner fhould ftudy to execute the two felect upper parades of the counter in carte and tierce in the moft juft and eafy manner, combining and uniting them as occafion may require, with any of the felect lower parades, flying from one to the other in purfuit of your adverfary's blade. Thefe, if well executed, will parry all your adverfay's feints and thrufts. When you make attacks upon him, advance to gain your meafure with glizades along his blade, beats of the foot, &c. execute the moft fimple and natural feints to deceive him in your intended thrufts, quickly recovering to avoid his return, *See practical variations in part 2, and obfervations interfperfed on the mode of attacking in part 3*, from which you may felect a few of the moft favourite feints, thrufts and other movements, and apply them with judgment in ferious affairs.

Of *Disarming*.

WHEN yon first engage seriously in the assault with an intention to disarm your adversary, keep out of measure, disengage nimbly from carte to tierce and from tierce to carte, so as he may not be aware of your designs; but advert never to disengage when you advance towards him, as it exposes you to the time thrust, &c. On the contrary, advance always on a firm and steady guard, gliding along his blade. Pay min e attention to the position of your adversary, that you may seize every favourable advantage: if you find his arm stiff, and somewhat stretched on guard, you should seize the opportunity of giving his blade a strong and abrupt beat on the feeble thereof in tierce, making a sudden reverse of the wrist with the nails downwards. It seldom fails in disarming your adversary; at any rate, will disconcert him, so as to render (almost to a certainty) any thrust that you may attempt against him effectual: please to observe to keep your arm always flexible upon guard, and your body in a proper side position, and it will conduce greatly in making your beat more powerful and abrupt, when attempting to disarm him in the above manner; besides by keeping your arm in a flexible posture, it will render all attempts that your adversary may make to disarm you ineffectual.

The above manner of disarming may be attempted with safety and advantage, after you have parried your adversary's thrust by simple carte, or the counter in carte, perceiving that he recovers with a stretched arm, in place of delivering a return, as he will naturally expect, disengage to tierce, and powerfully beat his blade, as already directed.

Another safe and advantageous manner of disarming your adversary is by crossing his sword, so as to twirl it out of his hand. It is generally performed after parrying your adversary's thrust by simple carte, or the counter

Disarming by Crossing the Sword.

ter in carte without quitting his blade, leaning abruptly thereon, and binding it with yours. Reverse your wrist, with the nails downwards, as if in seconde, and with the motion thereof give his blade an abrupt twirl, which, if it does not disarm him, will throw his hand and blade out of the line of direction, so as you may effectually fix your point, and deliver him a thrust in seconde. (*See plate* 19.)

After parrying your adversary's thrust by simple tierce, or the counter in tierce; you may also cross his sword before he recovers; make a strong and abrupt circular movement with your wrist in seconde, without quitting his blade; and it will either disarm, or give you an opening to deliver him a thrust. *(See plate* 19.*)*

Besides, in serious affairs, if you are inclined to disable your adversary, or cause him to lose his sword, out of measure you may perform a few low feints, if you find that he will use semicircle, when you mark the feint of low carte and octave when you counter disengage;

engage, after marking the feint in low carte, you should pretend to counter disengage to octave; but deceive him by only half disengaging, and as he forms his parade in octave, quickly gain your measure, and make a straight thrust to his wrist or hand, by extending your arm, or forming the compleat extension. If the point of your sword is well fixed and directed, it will disable your adversary by touching him in the wrist, or running in between the thumb and first finger. You should be always prepared to parry, and remove your body with agility out of measure, after attempting the above method of disabling your adversary; simple octave, or the counter in octave, should be quickly formed, after making such an attempt, so as to guard against any thrusts he may deliver.

To perform all the above methods of disarming with nicety, requires a powerful command and flexibility of the wrist; which you may in a short time acquire, by paying proper attention to the practice of the foils. In practising with foils, the above method of disarming, by abruptly crossing the blade, please to observe not to

rely

rely upon any aid the button of your adverfary's foil may give you in feizing the feeble of his blade, and in fuddenly reverfing your wrift. That is a falfe method of practifing this difarm, and may be attended with bad confequences, if attempted in ferious affairs.

The antient fyftem of difarming, by advancing and feizing your adverfary's arm in various pofitions, &c. together with plungeons, voltes, &c. are now entirely exploded; as they were found impracticable fword-in-hand, without putting the perfon who might attempt them in eminent danger of lofing his life. Therefore, I have paffed them over in filence, and have only made a few obfervations on the moft eligible method of difarming your adverfary in ferious affairs.

F I N I S.